Vergil's Aeneid

Selected Readings
from Books 1, 2, 4, and 6

TEACHER'S GUIDE

by Barbara Weiden Boyd

Bolchazy-Carducci Publishers, Inc.
Mundelein, Illinois USA

Editor: Bridget Buchholz
Design & Layout: Adam Phillip Velez
Cover Illustration: Detail from "Inside the gate" by Thom Kapheim

Vergil's *Aeneid*: Selected Readings from Books 1, 2, 4, and 6
Teacher's Guide

Barbara Weiden Boyd

The selections and notes from Books 1, 2, 4, and 6 are fully revised from *Vergil's AENEID,
Books I–VI*, by Clyde Pharr (Bolchazy-Carducci Publishers, 1998).

The Latin text is from *P. Vergili Maronis Opera* (Oxford, 1969; repr. with corrections, 1972)
R. A. B. Mynors, ed., by permission of Oxford University Press.

Advanced Placement® and AP® are trademarks registered and/or owned by the College
Board, which was not involved in the production of, and does not endorse, this product.

© 2012 Bolchazy-Carducci Publishers, Inc.
All rights reserved.

Bolchazy-Carducci Publishers, Inc.
1570 Baskin Road
Mundelein, Illinois 60060
www.bolchazy.com

Printed in the United States of America
2016
by Publishers' Graphics

ISBN 978-0-86516-766-7

Contents

Introduction

The contents of this supplementary volume are meant to serve as aids to teachers and to students working independently on the *Aeneid*. The literal translation is just that: I have attempted to reflect in English as much as possible the syntax and structure of Vergil's Latin and have studiously attempted not to obscure the difficulty of some of Vergil's language. I have maintained the tenses of the verbs as they appear in Latin, although this may sound ungainly to the reader not long familiar with this flexible feature of literary Latin. When I have found it necessary to supplement the translation with occasional words or phrases to clarify the sense of a given passage, I have put the supplementary material in square brackets; parentheses are used only where they appear in the printed Latin text as well.

The list of questions for discussion and analysis is meant to help teachers and readers new to the passages covered in the companion volume by encouraging thoughtfulness about the readings and provoking discussion. I rarely consider one and only one answer to be the "right" one; rather, I encourage all my readers to take these questions as a starting point for open-ended and, I hope, productive discussion. These questions are not by any means the only ones that can be asked about the passages considered here, and I encourage my readers to develop questions of their own to pose. The texts under consideration ably demonstrate the inherent wealth of Vergil's creativity, capable of stirring anew emotion and thoughtfulness in each subsequent generation. I am delighted to have the opportunity to make this wealth more accessible to my readers.

This Teacher's Guide also includes a "clean" copy of the Latin text based on R. A. B. Mynors' 1969 edition of the Oxford Classical Text, free of the special formatting used in the textbook (i.e., mixed typefaces and macrons). Teachers are encouraged to incorporate this text into classwork and tests so that students will be prepared for the appearance of the text on the actual AP exam, and of other Latin texts they may encounter in college courses or elsewhere. As always, I encourage teachers to remind students that macrons were not written in ancient texts, but are a modern linguistic and pedagogical device. The "clean" text is meant to help students and teachers alike experience Vergil's poem with as little editorial intrusion as possible.

BARBARA WEIDEN BOYD
Bowdoin College

A Literal Translation of Vergil's *Aeneid* Selected Readings from Books 1, 2, 4, and 6

Note: Words and phrases in square brackets are generally supplements to (or, in a very few cases, subtractions from) the Latin text, intended in all cases to clarify for the reader Vergil's meaning. Parentheses are used only where they appear in the Latin text (OCT), or where there would otherwise be double brackets.

Book 1
Aeneid 1.1–209

1.1–33

I sing of arms and of the man who first [as] an exile from the shores of Troy, because of fate, came to Italy and the Lavinian shores; that man [having been] tossed about a great deal both on land and at sea by the power of the gods, on account of the unforgetting wrath of cruel Juno, and having endured much also in war, until he could found a city and bring [his] gods into Latium; whence [i.e., from this origin] [came] the Latin people and the Alban fathers and the walls of lofty Rome. Muse, recall to me the reasons: with what divine power having been wounded [i.e., as the result of harm done to what divine power] or grieving at what did the queen of the gods compel a man outstanding in devotion [i.e., to gods, home, and family] to endure so many misfortunes, confront so many struggles? Do the heavenly spirits possess wrath[s] of such magnitude?

There was an ancient city (Tyrian settlers possessed it), Carthage, far opposite Italy and the mouth[s] of the Tiber, rich in resources and most fierce in the pursuits of war, which alone Juno is said to have cherished more than all [other] lands, preferred even to Samos [lit., Samos being held in second place]. Here [were] her weapons, here was [her] chariot; the queen even now intends and nurtures this [place] to be the kingdom [i.e., ruling power] for [its] peoples, if the fates should permit [this] in any way. But indeed she had heard that offspring which would one day overturn the Tyrian citadel[s] was being produced from Trojan blood; from this [i.e., offspring or event] would come a people ruling broadly and proud in war for the destruction of Libya; [and had heard that] the Fates were unrolling [the destiny of Carthage] thus. The Saturnian, fearing this and mindful of the old war, because she had first [or formerly] waged [war] at Troy on behalf of her beloved Argives—and not even yet had the causes of her wrath[s] and her cruel sorrows fallen from [her] mind; buried in [her] deep mind [i.e., buried deep in her mind] remains the judgment of Paris and the insult to her rejected beauty and the hated people and the honors of [i.e., given to] stolen Ganymede [or the stolen honors of Ganymede]: inflamed on account of these things, she was keeping far off from Latium the Trojans, tossed about upon the entire sea, the remnants of [i.e., left by] the Greeks and cruel Achilles, and they were wandering for many years, driven by the fates around all the seas. [Of] so great a struggle was it to found the Roman people.

1.34–49

Scarcely out of sight of the Sicilian land the men happily [lit., the happy men] were setting sail onto the deep [sea] and were plowing the foam of the salt [sea] with their bronze [i.e., their bronze-tipped prows], when Juno, preserving the everlasting wound under her breast [*or* deep in her heart,] [said] these things with [i.e., to] herself: "Am I, having been defeated, to cease from [my] undertaking, and to not be able to turn away from Italy the king of the Teucrians [i.e., Trojans]? Of course, I am prevented by the fates. Was Pallas [Minerva] able to burn up the fleet of the Argives and to drown the men themselves in the sea on account of the insult and madness of one man, Ajax son of Oileus? She herself, having hurled the swift fire of Jupiter from the clouds, both scattered the ships and overturned the sea with the winds, and him she snatched up in a whirlwind [as he was] breathing out flames from his transfixed breast, and she impaled [him] on a sharp crag. But I, who proceed as queen of the gods and both sister and wife of Jupiter, have been waging war [lit., do wage war] with a single people for so many years [now]. And who will worship [lit., worships] the divinity of Juno hereafter or, [as] a suppliant, will place an offering on [her] altars?"

1.50–80

Pondering such things with [*or* to] herself in her inflamed heart, the goddess comes to the the country of the clouds, a place teeming with the raging south winds, Aeolia. Here in his vast cave king Aeolus controls with authority the struggling winds and howling storms and reins [them] in with the restraints of [his] prison [lit., with chains and with prison]. Chafing, they rumble around the barriers [i.e., the prison containing them] with a great roar of the mountain; Aeolus sits on his lofty citadel holding his scepter[s], and he both soothes [their] spirits and calms [their] wrath[s]. Were he not to do [this], the swift [winds] would surely carry off with themselves the seas and lands and the deep heaven, and would sweep [them] through the air. But fearing this, the all-powerful father hid [them] in dark caves, and set above [them] a mass and lofty mountains [i.e., a mass of lofty mountains], and gave them a [i.e., the sort of] king who would know both how to restrain [them] by means of a clear agreement and how, [when] ordered, to give loose reins [i.e, slacken his hold on the reins.] To him then Juno [as] suppliant employed these words:

"Aeolus (since the father of gods and king of men granted to you [the ability] to soothe the waves and to raise [them] with the wind), a people hostile to me sails the Tyrrhenian sea, carrying Troy and [its or their] conquered household gods into Italy. Strike violence into the winds and overwhelm the submerged ships [i.e., overwhelm and submerge the ships], or drive [the Trojans] in different directions and scatter their bodies on the sea. There are [in my possession] twice seven nymphs of outstanding physical beauty, of whom Deiopea, who is most beautiful in form [or There are in my possession twice seven Nymphs of outstanding beauty; she who is the the most beautiful of these in form, Deiopea], I shall join [to you] in stable marriage and shall declare your own, so that she may live [lit., carry through] all her years with you in return for such merits [i.e., in return for this favor] and so that she may make you a father of fair offspring."

Aeolus [spoke] these words in response: "[It is] your task, queen, to search out what you wish; for me it is right to undertake what has been ordered [lit., the ordered things]. Whatever [of] kingdom this is you win over for me, you unite [to me] the scepter[s] [i.e., of power] and Jupiter, you grant [to me] to recline at the feasts of the gods and you make [me] the one ruling [i.e., the ruler of] clouds and storms."

1.81–123

When these [words had been] said, he struck the hollow mountain against its side with [his] spear reversed [*or* reversed spear]; and the winds rush forth, just as [when] a battle line [has been] drawn up [lit., a battle-line having been drawn up], where a gateway [is] given, and they blow through the lands in a whirlwind [*or* in the manner of a whirlwind]. [Now] they brooded over the sea, and the East wind and South wind together, and the Southwest wind thick with squalls, heave up the whole [sea] from [its] deep foundations, and roll huge waves toward the shores. The shouting of men and the grating of the ropes follow[s]; suddenly the clouds snatch both the sky and day [i.e., daylight] out of the eyes [i.e., sight] of the Teucrians [i.e., Trojans]; black night broods over the sea; and the poles thundered and the upper air flashes with frequent [bursts of] fires, and everything threatens the men with imminent death [lit., all things aim imminent death at the men].

Suddenly Aeneas' limbs are loosened with cold [i.e., fear]; he groans, and outstretching to the stars his two hands he says such things with [his] voice: "O three and four times fortunate, [those] to whom it befell to encounter [death] before the faces of [their] fathers beneath the lofty walls of Troy! O son of Tydeus, strongest of the people of the Danaans! Could I not have fallen on the Trojan plains and poured forth this soul at [i.e., by means of] your right hand, where fierce Hector lies because of the spear of the grandson of Aeacus [i.e., Achilles], where huge Sarpedon [lies], where the river Simois rolls beneath [its] waves so many snatched shields of men, and [their] helmets and brave bodies?"

As he was [lit., to him] uttering such things, a roaring gust from the North wind strikes the sail head-on, and raises the waves to the stars. The oars are broken, then the prow turns away and offers the side [of the ship] to the waves, [and] a towering mountain of water pursues in a mass. These men [i.e., some men] hang on the top of a wave; a gaping wave reveals the earth among the waves for these [i.e., other men], [and] the surge rages in the [*or* with] sand[s]. The South wind whirls three [ships] [that have been] snatched up onto the lurking rocks (the rocks in the middle of the waves which the Italians call "Altars," a huge ridge on the surface of the sea), the East wind drives three [ships] from the deep onto the shallows and reefs, wretched to see, and dashes [them] on the shoals and encircles them with a mound of sand. One [i.e., of the ships], which was carrying the Lycians and trusty Orontes, the huge sea from high above beats against the prow before the eyes of him himself [i.e., before Aeneas' eyes]; and the pilot is struck out [of the ship] face-first and rolls headlong, but the wave, driving that [ship] around three times, whirls it in the same place, and the swift whirlpool swallows [it] up in the sea. Men appear here and there [lit., scattered] swimming in the vast whirlpool, the weapons of men and planks [i.e., of the ship] and Trojan treasure [scattered] through the waves. Now the storm has overcome the strong ship of Ilioneus, now [that] of brave Achates, and [the ship] on which Abas [was] carried, and [that] on which aged Aletes [was carried]; the seams of the sides having been loosened [i.e., since the seams of the ships' sides had become loose], they all [i.e., all the ships] take on hostile water and gape with cracks.

1.124–56

Meanwhile, Neptune, gravely disturbed, sensed that the sea was being confused with a great rumbling and that a storm [had been] sent forth and that the still waters [had been] poured back from [*or* to] the depths of the sea, and looking out over the deep sea he raised [his] peaceful head from the top of the water. He sees the fleet of Aeneas scattered on the entire sea, [and] the Trojans overwhelmed by waves and by the downfall of heaven; nor did the tricks and wrath of Juno escape the notice of [her] brother. He calls the East and West winds to himself, [and] thereupon speaks such things: "Has so great a confidence in your origin taken hold of you? Do you dare now, winds, to stir up heaven and earth without my divine power and to raise such great masses [i.e., of confusion]? [You] whom I—but it is better to compose the waves [that have been] disturbed. Afterwards you will atone for your crimes to me with a different [lit., not similar] punishment. Speed [your] flight and say these things to your king: not to him [has been] given by lot the rule of the sea and the cruel trident, but to me. He possesses huge rocks, your home[s], East wind; let Aeolus toss himself about in that hall and rule, after the winds have been shut in their prison [lit., with the prison of the winds having been shut]." Thus he speaks, and more swiftly than speech [lit., than a word] he calms the swollen seas and puts the assembled clouds to flight and brings back the sun. Together Cymothoe and Triton, pushing, dislodge the ships from the sharp rock; he himself [i.e., Neptune] raises [them] with [his] trident and reveals the huge sandbars and calms the sea and glides along the top of the waves with swift wheels. And just as when, as often [i.e., as often happens], a riot has begun in a great populace, and the common crowd rages in spirit[s] [*or* with anger] and now torches and rocks fly,

[and] madness supplies weapons; then, if by chance they catch sight [lit., have caught sight] of any man solemn in devotion and service[s], they fall silent and stand with [their] ears pricked up [lit., their ears having been raised]; he rules their minds with [his] words and soothes [their] hearts: thus subsided the entire uproar of the sea, after the father, looking out on the seas and conveyed in the open sky, guides [his] horses and gives rein, flying along, to [his] obedient chariot.

1.157–209

Exhausted, the followers of Aeneas struggle to seek the shores which [are] closest on [their] course [*or* with haste], and are turned [i.e, turn] to the coasts of Libya. There is a place in a long recess: an island creates a port with the projection of [its] sides, by [means of] which every wave from the deep is broken, and splits itself into recessed bays. From this side and from that, vast crags and twin cliffs [extending] into the sky tower, beneath the summit of which the safe waters are silent far and wide; then from above [there is] a stage set with quivering woods, and a black grove threatens with bristling shade. Under the opposite face [there is] a cave [made out] of suspended stone; within [there are] sweet waters and seats [made out] of the living rock, the home of the nymphs. Here no chains hold exhausted ships, no anchor binds [them] with its hooked bite. Aeneas enters this place with seven ships gathered from the entire number [i.e., of ships], and, disembarking, the Trojans take possession of the longed-for sand with a great love for land, and set [their] bodies [lit., limbs] dripping with salt [i.e., saltwater] on the shore.

And first of all, Achates struck a spark from a flint, and took up the fire with leaves, and gave around [i.e., scattered] dry nourishment[s] [i.e., kindling], and caught the flame in the tinder. Then the men, exhausted from the events [i.e., the storm], prepare the grain [lit., Ceres] spoiled by the waters and the tools for preparing the grain, and they prepare to roast the recovered grain[s] with flames and to grind [it] with stone.

Meanwhile, Aeneas climbs the cliff, and seeks all the view far and wide on the sea, if [i.e., in the hope that] he may see any [sign of] Antheus tossed by the wind, and the Phrygian biremes, or Capys, or the weapons of Caicus on the high prow[s]. He sees no ship in sight, [but] three stags wandering on the shore; entire herds follow them from the rear and the long line grazes through [the length of] the valleys. He took a stand here and snatched with [his] hand the bow and swift arrows, the weapons which loyal Achates was carrying, and first lays low the leaders [of the herd] themselves bearing heads lofty with tree-like antlers, then he confuses the herd and the entire crowd, driving [them] with [his] weapons among the leafy groves. Nor does he stop before, [as] victor, he lays low seven huge bodies on the ground and matches their number with [that of] the ships. From here, he seeks the port, and divides [the spoils] among all [his] companions. He distributes the wine which the good hero Acestes had then [i.e., when still back at Sicily] loaded in jars on the Sicilian shore and had given them as they were departing [lit., to the departing ones], and he soothes [their] grieving hearts with words:

"O companions (for neither are we ignorant of troubles before), o men having suffered more severe things, the god will give a limit to these [things], too. You have both approached the Scyllaean rage and the deeply resounding cliffs, and you [have] experienced the Cyclopian rocks. Call back your spirits and let go of sorrowful fear; perhaps at some time [in the future] it will be pleasing to remember even these things. We head into Latium, where the fates show [us] quiet home[s], through varied misfortunes, through so many dangers of things. There it is right for the kingdom of Troy to rise again. Endure, and save yourselves for favorable conditions." He says such things with [his] voice, and [though] sick with huge cares he feigns hope on [his] face, [and] presses his grief deep in his heart.

AENEID 1.418–40

1.418–40

Meanwhile, they took up the road, wherever the path shows [itself], and presently they were climbing the hill, which looms very great over the city, and which looks from above at the citadels opposite. Aeneas marvels at the mass [or construction] [i.e., of the city], formerly huts, [and] marvels at the gates and the noise and the beds of roads. Burning [i.e., with eagerness] the Tyrians press on: some extended [or were eager to extend] the walls and fortified [or were eager to fortify] the citadel and rolled rocks up[hill] with [their] hands, some chose [or were eager to choose] a place for a building and enclosed [or were eager to enclose] it with a furrow; they select laws and magistracies and a revered senate. Here, some excavate the ports; here, others place the lofty foundations for theaters, and cut huge columns out of the cliffs, tall adornments for future stages. Just as work busies the bees under the sun in early summer through flowery country regions, when they bring forth the full-grown offspring of the race, or when they stuff the dripping honey [i.e., into the comb] and stretch the cells with sweet nectar, or receive the burdens of those coming, or, lined up in a row [lit., a line having been made], they ward off the drones, a lazy bunch [lit., swarm], from the hives; the work heats up and the fragrant honey smells of thyme. "O fortunate ones, whose walls now rise!" says Aeneas, and he looks up at the heights of the city. He bears himself along wrapped in a cloud (marvelous to tell!) through their midst, and mixes with the men and is not seen by anyone.

Aeneid 1.494–578

1.494–519

While these things appear to Dardanian Aeneas to be marvelled at, while he stands agape and clings fastened on one view, the queen proceeds to the temple, Dido, most beautiful in appearance, with a great band of youths thronging about. Just as [when] Diana trains [her] choruses on the banks of Eurotas or along the ridges of Cynthus, [Diana] whom a thousand mountain nymphs follow [lit., having followed] and are gathered from this side and that: she bears a quiver on her shoulder and, stepping, surpasses all the [other] goddesses (joys possess the silent heart of Latona): such was Dido, so she carried herself, happy, urging on the work and the future kingdoms through the midst [of those about her]. Then at the doors of the goddess, in the middle of the vault of the temple, surrounded by weapons and resting high on her throne she sat. She gave rights and laws to men, and she equalized the labor of the works in equal parts or drew [the work assignments] by lot—when suddenly Aeneas sees approaching in a great crowd Antheus and Sergestus and brave Cloanthus and others of the Trojans, whom the black whirlwind at sea had driven apart and had deep within carried to other shores. At once he himself stood agape, at once Achates [was] struck with both happiness and fear; eager, they burned [with desire] to join right [hands]; but the unknown situation disturbs [their] minds. They disguise [their eagerness] and, enclosed in a hollow cloud, they watch [to learn] what fate the men have [lit., what fate (there is) to the men], on what shore they are leaving the fleet, why they are coming; for having been chosen from all the ships they went begging [i.e., to beg] a favor and sought the temple with a shout.

1.520–33

After they entered and the opportunity for speaking openly [was] given, greatest Ilioneus began thus in a peaceful manner [lit., with a peaceful heart]: "O queen, to whom Jupiter has granted [the ability] to establish a new city and to rein in proud peoples with justice, we wretched Trojans, having been carried across all the seas by the winds, beseech you: keep the unspeakable fire[s] from [our] ships, spare [our] devoted people, and attend more closely to our affairs. We have not come either to lay waste the Libyan household gods with the sword [lit., iron] or to divert stolen booty to the shores; this violence [does] not [exist] in [our] mind nor [is there] such haughtiness in the conquered. There is a place, the Greeks call [it] Hesperia by name/nickname, an ancient land, powerful in arms and in the fertility of the soil; Oenotrian men cultivated it; now the rumor [is] that [their] younger ones/descendants called the people 'Italy' from [i.e., after] the name of [their] leader.

1.534–60

[Our] route was here, when suddenly, cloudy Orion, rising up from the wave, carried us onto the unseen shoals and thoroughly, with the South winds [being] bold, scattered [us] both through the waves, with the sea-swell overpowering [us], and through the pathless rocks; hither we few have sailed to your shores. What [is] this kind/race of people? Or what so barbarous a country allows this custom? We are kept from the hospitality of the sand; they raise wars and forbid [us] to set foot on the first land [i.e., forbid us to so much as set foot on their land]. If you have no thought for the human race and mortal weapons, hope at least that the gods are mindful of what should be said and what should not be said [i.e., of right and wrong]. Aeneas was king to us, than whom no other was more just, neither in devotion, nor greater in war and arms. If the fates preserve this man, if he lives on ethereal air and does not yet lie in the cruel shadows, there is no fear [for us], nor should it shame you to have strived to be first in service. There are cities in Sicilian regions, too, and weapons, and famous Acestes, from Trojan blood. Let it be permitted to lead up/land [our] fleet shattered by the winds, and to shape lumber from the forests and to trim [branches into] oars, if it is permitted to head for Italy with [our] comrades and leader restored, so that we may happily seek Italy and Latium; but if salvation [has been] lost, and the sea of Libya holds you, best father of the Trojans, and the hope of Iulus no longer remains, yet at least let us seek the seas of Sicily and the homes/settlement prepared [for us there], from where we [have] come here, and [let us seek] king Acestes." With such [words spoke] Ilioneus; all the descendants of Dardanus roared together with speech/mouth.

1.561–78

Dido, having lowered her face, then speaks out briefly: "Loosen the fear from [your] heart[s], Trojans, set aside [your] cares. The difficult situation and the newness of [my] rule compel me to construct such things [i.e., fortifications] and to protect [my] territory with guard[s] far and wide. Who does not know of the people of the descendants of Aeneas, who [does not know of] the city of Troy, both [its] courage and [its] men, or the fires of so great a war? We Phoenicians do not have such dulled hearts, nor does the Sun yoke [his] horses so far from the Tyrian city. Whether you desire great Hesperia and the Saturnian fields or the regions of Eryx and king Acestes, I shall send [you] away safe with [my] help and shall assist [you] with resources. Do you wish to settle equally with me in these kingdoms? The city which I am establishing is yours; pull [your] ships up [i.e., onto the shore]; Trojan and Tyrian will be led by me with no distinction. And if only king Aeneas himself were present, driven by the same South wind! Indeed, I will send out men I can be sure of [lit., sure men] along the shores and will order [them] to survey the borders of Libya, [to see] if, having been tossed out [from his ship], he is wandering in any forests or towns."

Book 2
Aeneid 2.40–56

2.40–56

Then first before [them] all, with a great band accompanying [him], Laocoon, ablaze [i.e., crazed with emotion] runs down from the highest citadel, and from afar [says]: 'O unfortunate citizens, what [is this] so great madness? Do you believe that the enemies [have been] carried away? Or do you think that any gifts of the Greeks are lacking in tricks? Thus is Ulysses known [i.e., is Ulysses famous for *not* being tricky]? Either the Greeks are hidden shut up in this lumber, or this device has been built [to go] against our walls, in order to look down upon [our] homes and to come upon the city from above, or some [other] trick lies hidden; do not trust in the horse, Teucrians [Trojans]. Whatever it is, I fear the Greeks, even [those] bearing gifts.' Having spoken thus, with mighty strength he hurled a huge spear into the flank and into the belly of the beast, curved with joints. That [spear] stood fixed, quivering, and in the shaken belly the hollow cavities resounded and gave a groan. And, if the fates of the gods, if [their] intention had not been ill-omened, he [would have] compelled [us] to defile the Argive hiding places with iron, and Troy would now stand, and you would remain, lofty citadel of Priam.

Aeneid 2.201–49

2.201–27

Laocoon, priest for Neptune chosen by lot, was sacrificing a huge bull at the solemn altars. But behold!—from Tenedos twin snakes with immense coils (I shudder recalling [this]) across the peaceful depths loom over the sea and head for the shores side by side; of which [i.e., of these] the breasts, raised [high] among the waves, and blood-red crests surmount the seas; the other part [i.e., of the snakes' bodies] skims the sea behind and twists the huge backs in a coil. [As] the salt-sea [is] foaming a sound is made; and now they were taking hold of the fields and, their blazing eyes suffused [lit., suffused in respect to their flaming eyes] with blood and fire, they licked their hissing mouths with vibrating tongues. Pale, we fled from the sight [*or* made pale at the sight, we fled]. Those [snakes] pursue Laocoon in a fixed line; and first of all, each serpent, having embraced the small bodies of the two sons [i.e., of Laocoon], entwines [them] and feeds on [the] pitiable limbs with [its] bite; afterwards, they seize [Laocoon] himself approaching as help and bearing weapons, and bind [him] with huge coils; and now, having wrapped him in the middle twice, twice having placed their scaly bodies around his neck, they tower over [him] with [their] head[s] and lofty necks. At that very moment that one [i.e., Laocoon] tries to pull apart the knots with [his] hands, his headbands soaked [lit., having been soaked with respect to his headbands] with gore and black poison, at that very moment he raises horrifying cries to the stars. Of such a sort [is] the mooing, when a wounded bull flees the altar and has shaken from [his] neck the ill-aimed axe. But in a glide [*or* by means of gliding] the twin snakes escape to the highest shrines and seek the citadel of the cruel Tritonian [i.e., Minerva], and beneath the feet of the goddess and beneath the circle of [her] shield they are hidden.

2.228–49

Then to be sure a new fear creeps through the terrified hearts in [us] all, and they say that Laocoon deserving[ly] paid for a crime [lit., deserving paid for a crime], who [because he] wounded the oak [i.e., the horse] with a lance and hurled a wicked spear into/at [the horse's] back. They shout in unison that the image is to be led to the seats [of the gods] and that the powers of the goddess are to be entreated.

We split the ramparts and spread open the walls of the city. All equip [themselves] for the task and put glidings of wheels [i.e., gliding wheels] beneath the feet [of the horse], and extend hempen cables from [*or* to] the neck; the deadly device scales the walls, pregnant with weapons. Boys and unwed girls sing holy things [i.e., sacred songs] around [the horse] and delight to touch the rope with [their] hand[s]; that [device] goes up and glides, threatening the middle of the city. O homeland! O Ilium, home of the gods, and Trojans' walls, famed in war! Four times on the threshold itself of the gate it resisted, and four times the weapons gave forth a sound from the belly; we press on nonetheless, heedless and blinded by madness, and we set the unlucky omen on the hallowed citadel. Even then for the purpose [*or* by means] of the fates to come Cassandra discloses words [lit., mouths] not ever, by the order of a god, believed by [us] Trojans. We unfortunates, for whom that day was to be the last, deck the shrines of the gods with festive foliage through the city.

AENEID 2.268–97

2.268–97

It was the time when first quiet begins for wretched mortals and, [as] a gift from the gods, creeps up, most pleasing[ly].—in sleep, most miserable Hector seemed to me to be present, before [my] eyes, and to pour out copious tears, as once [he was] dragged by [the] two-horse chariot, and black with bloody dust and pierced [with] a thong through his swollen feet. Woe to me! Of such a sort was he, how much changed from that Hector who returned clothed in the spoils of Achilles, or having flung Phrygian fire[s] on the ships of the Danaans [Greeks]; bearing a filthy beard, and locks matted with blood, and those wounds, a very great number of which he received around [his] homeland's walls. Weeping voluntarily, I myself seemed to address the man and to bring forth mournful words: 'O light of Troy, O most faithful hope of the Teucrians [Trojans], what so great delays have kept [you]? From what shores do you come, Hector, eagerly awaited? How [gladly] we, exhausted, look upon you, after many deaths of your people, after the various struggles of men and of the city! What undeserved cause has befouled [your] peaceful countenance[s]? Or why do I see these wounds?' He [answered] nothing, nor does he delay me asking empty things [i.e., vainly], but grievously drawing groans from his deep heart he says, 'Alas, [child] born from a goddess, flee, and snatch yourself from these flames. The enemy holds the ramparts; Troy rushes downward from [its] lofty summit. Enough [has been] given to the homeland and to Priam; if Troy were able to be defended by [any] hand, it would indeed have been defended by this [one]. Troy entrusts [her] holy things [i.e., rituals] and her household gods to you; take these [as] companions of [your] fates, seek for these great walls, which you will establish at last, the sea having been thoroughly wandered.' Thus he speaks, and with his hands he carries forth from the innermost sanctuaries the headbands and powerful Vesta and the eternal flame.

AENEID 2.559–620

2.559–66

But then for the first time harsh dread surrounded me. I stood in a daze; the image of [my] dear father rose up, as I saw the king, equal in age, breathing out [his] life because of [*or* from] a cruel wound, [the image of] abandoned Creusa and the forsaken house and the misfortune of little Iulus rose up. I look back and survey what abundance [i.e., of forces] is around me. Worn out, all [had] deserted [me], and with a leap [had] sent [their] wretched bodies to the earth or [had] given [them] to the fires.

2.567–76

And now indeed I alone was surviving, when I see the daughter of Tyndarus [i.e., Helen] keeping the thresholds of Vesta and silent[ly] lurking in a remote place. The fires give a bright light to me wandering and carrying [my] eyes through everything all about. That one, the shared Fury [i.e., destructive force] of Troy and of [her] homeland, fearing beforehand the Trojans hostile to her on account of Troy [having been] overturned and the punishment of [i.e., from] the Greeks and the wrath[s] of [her] abandoned husband, had hidden herself and, hateful, was sitting at the altar[s]. Fires flared up in [my] mind; wrath arises to avenge the falling country and to exact wicked penalties.

2.577–87

'To be sure, will this woman, unharmed, look upon Sparta and ancestral Mycenae, and will she proceed [as] a queen, a triumph having been produced? Will she see [her] marriage and the home of [her] father and [her] children, accompanied by a throng of Trojan women and by Phrygian attendants? Will Priam have fallen by the sword? Will Troy have burned with fire? Will the Dardanian shore have sweated so often with blood? [It will *or* Let it] not [be] so. For although there is no glorious reputation in the punishment of a woman, this victory holds praise; I shall be praised nevertheless to have extinguished an unspeakable thing and to have exacted deserving penalties, and it will be pleasing to have fulfilled [my] intent and to have satiated the ashes of my people †the reputation of an avenger†.'

2.588–93

I was uttering such things and was being borne along with enraged mind, when [my] nurturing parent presented herself to me to be seen, previously not so clear to [my] eyes, and shone through the night in the pure light having revealed the goddess and both of what sort and of what size she is accustomed to appear to the heaven-dwellers, and checked [me], having been seized, with [her] right [hand], and added these things in addition from [her] rosy mouth:

2.594–603

'Son, what so great grief arouses unrestrained wrath(s)? Why do you rage? Or to where has your care for us [i.e., for me] withdrawn? Will you not first see where you have left [your] father Anchises, weary with age, whether [your] wife Creusa survives, and [your] boy Ascanius? Around all of whom [i.e., all of them] Greek troops wander on all sides, and unless my care resisted, by now the hostile flames would have borne [them away] and the sword would have drained [them (i.e., of life)]. The hated face of the Lacaenian daughter of Tyndarus or Paris [is] not [to be] blamed by you; the mercilessness of the gods, of the gods, overturns these riches and lays low Troy from [its] height.

2.604–20

Look (for I shall remove every cloud which, drawn around you as you watch, now dulls mortal sight[s], and damp[ly] darkens around [you]; you, do not fear any commands of your parent nor decline to obey the orders [lit., what has been bidden]): here, where you see the scattered (i.e., destroyed) structures and the rocks torn from rocks, and the smoke swelling with dust mixed in, Neptune shakes the walls and the foundations, dislodged with a great trident, and tears the whole city from its base[s]. Here, most cruel Juno in front [lit., first] holds the Scaean gates and, raging, girded with iron [i.e., a sword], calls the allied troop from the ships. Look back, even now Tritonian Pallas occupies the highest citadels, gleaming forth from a cloud and with the cruel Gorgon. The father himself [i.e., Jupiter] supplies spirits and favorable strength to the Greeks, he himself stirs the gods against Trojan arms. Son, seize [the opportunity for] flight and place a limit on [your] struggle; nowhere will I be absent, and I will set you, safe, on your ancestral threshold.'

Book 4
AENEID 4.160–218

4.160–72

Meanwhile, the heaven begins to be confused with a great rumble, a storm-cloud follows with hail mixed in, and in all directions the Tyrian comrades and the Trojan youth and the Dardanian descendant of Venus [i.e., Ascanius] in fear sought different covers [i.e., places of cover] through the fields; the streams rush down from the mountains. Dido and the Trojan leader arrive at the same cave. Earth first and attendant Juno give a signal; fires and the upper air, witness to the union, flashed, and the nymphs shrieked on the highest peak. That day [was] the first [cause] of death and the first cause of evils; for neither by appearance nor by reputation is Dido moved, nor does she now ponder a secret love; she calls [this] marriage, she cloaks [her] fault with this name.

4.173–218

Immediately Rumor goes through the great cities of Libya, Rumor, than which no other evil [lit., bad thing] is swifter: she thrives on movement and acquires strength by going, small at first on account of fear, [but] soon she raises herself into the air[s] and steps on the earth and hides [her] head among the clouds. Parent Earth, as they report, provoked by wrath for the gods, gave birth to that [one] last [i.e., of the gods], a sister to Coeus and Enceladus, swift in respect to [her] feet and with swift wings, a dreadful portent, huge; as many feathers as there are to her [lit., to whom] with respect to her body, [there are] so many wakeful eyes beneath (marvelous to tell), as many tongues, as many mouths resound, she raises as many ears. At night she flies in the middle of [i.e., between] heaven and earth, rustling through the shadow, nor does she turn down [her] eyes in sweet sleep; in the light she sits [as] a guardian either at the top of the highest roof or in tall towers, and terrorizes great cities, as greedy a messenger of the false and perverse as of the true. This one, then, rejoicing, filled the peoples with varied talk, and proclaimed equally things done and undone: that Aeneas, born from Trojan blood, had come, to whom as husband fair Dido deigns to join herself; that now through the winter, however long it may be, they caress each other in luxury, forgetful of [their] kingdoms and seized with shameful desire. The loathsome goddess spreads these things everywhere to the mouths of men. Straightaway she turns her path[s] to king Iarbas, and inflames his mind with words and increases [his] anger[s].

This one, born from Ammon, a Garamantian nymph having been raped, [erected] a hundred huge temples to Jove in [his] broad kingdoms, erected a hundred altars, and with the blood of sheep had consecrated the watchful fire, eternal sentinel[s] of the gods, the fertile earth, and the thresholds flowering with varied wreaths. And crazed of mind and inflamed by bitter rumor, this one is said to have beseeched Jupiter greatly [lit., many things] [as] a suppliant, with hands upturned before the altars in the midst of the presence[s] of the gods: "All-powerful Jupiter, to whom now the Maurusian [i.e., Moorish] people, having dined on embroidered couches, pour [as a libation] Lenaean [i.e., Bacchic] honor [i.e., wine, the manifestation of Bacchus], do you see these things? Or, father, when you hurl [your] lightning bolts, do we quake at you in vain, and do blind fires in the clouds terrify the minds [of men] and stir up empty rumblings? The woman who, wandering in our territories, set up a small city at a price, to whom [we gave] a shore for plowing and to whom we gave the laws of the place, has rejected our marriage alliances and has received Aeneas [as] master into [her] kingdoms. And now, that Paris, with [his] effeminate retinue, having tied a Maeonian cap on [i.e., under] his chin and perfumed hair [lit., having been tied below his chin and perfumed hair with the Maeonian cap], has possession of the object taken; we, to be sure, bring gifts to your temples, and cherish an empty rumor."

AENEID 4.259–361

4.259–95

As soon as he touched the huts with [his] winged soles [i.e., feet], he spies Aeneas building citadels and making shelters. And to that one there was [i.e., he had] a sword spangled with tawny jasper, and a cloak let down from his shoulders was bright with Tyrian purple, which wealthy Dido had made [as] a gift, and she had separated the webs [i.e., she had woven into the fabric] with slender gold [thread]. Straightaway he addresses [him]: "Are you now laying the foundations of lofty Carthage and, wife-ruled, do you build up a lovely city? Alas, [you], having forgotten the kingdom and your affairs! The ruler himself of the gods, who turns the heaven and lands with [his] power, sends me to you from bright Olympus; he himself orders [me] to bear these commands through the swift breezes: What are you planning? Or with what expectation do you waste times of idleness in Libyan lands? If no glory of such great affairs moves you [and in addition you yourself do not pursue an effort on behalf of your own praise], consider Ascanius rising up and the hopes for [your] heir Iulus, to whom the kingdom of Italy and the Roman land is owed." Having spoken with such a speech the Cyllenean left mortal view[s] in the middle of [his] speech and from afar disappeared from [Aeneas'] eyes into thin air.

But Aeneas stood speechless indeed, frenzied at/by the sight, and [his] hair stood on end from horror and [his] voice stuck in [his] jaws. He is eager to depart in flight and to leave the sweet lands, stunned by so great a warning and order of the gods. Alas—what should he do? With what [form of] address should he dare to conciliate the raging queen? What first beginnings should he take up? And he divides his swift mind now in this direction now in that, and takes [it] into different directions and revolves [it] through all things. This opinion seemed preferable to him as he wavered [lit., to him wavering]: he calls Mnestheus and Sergestus and strong Serestus, [and orders them to] [lit., that they should] silent[ly] make ready the fleet and drive [their] companions to the shores, prepare weapons and conceal what the reason is for doing things anew; [he decides that] meanwhile, since excellent Dido does not know and does not expect such love[s] to be broken, he himself will test approaches and what times for speaking [are] easiest, what way [is] right for things. Very swiftly all glad[ly] obey the command and fulfill the orders.

4.296–330

But the queen suspects tricks (who could deceive a lover?), and was the first to understand movements about to come, fearing all things, [even] safe ones. The same wicked Rumor brought [to her], raving, [the news that] the fleet was being armed and the way was being prepared. Bereft of [her] mind she rages and rushes, inflamed, through the whole city, like a Bacchant aroused, rituals having been stirred up, when the triennial rites spur her, [the cry] "Bacchus" having been heard, and nocturnal Cithaeron calls [her] with a shout. Finally, she addresses Aeneas voluntarily with these words:

"Treacherous one, did you hope to pretend still that so great a crime was possible and to depart from my land quiet[ly]? Does neither our love, nor the right [hand] once given, nor Dido, about to die from a cruel death, hold you? Aren't you hurrying, in fact, to prepare the fleet under the winter star and to go through the deep in the midst of the North winds, cruel man? What, if you were not seeking foreign fields and unknown homes, and ancient Troy remained, would Troy be sought by the fleets through the wave-filled sea? Are you fleeing me? By these tears and your right hand (since I myself have left nothing else to my now-wretched self), by our marriage[s], by the wedding hymns begun, if I have well deserved anything regarding you, or anything of mine was sweet to you, pity the falling house and discard, I beg you, that intention of yours, if [there is] any place still for prayers. On account of you the Libyan peoples and the rulers of the Nomads hate [me and] the Tyrians [are] hostile; on account of the same you, [my sense of] shame [has been] extinguished, and my earlier reputation, by which alone I was approaching the stars. For what do you, guest (since this name alone remains from [my] husband), desert me, about to die? Why do I delay? Or [am I waiting] until [my] brother Pygmalion destroys my city walls, or Gaetulian Iarbas takes [me] captive? At least, if there had been some progeny begotten to me from you before flight, if some little Aeneas were playing for me in the hall, who at least recalled you in face, I would not indeed seem entirely taken and forsaken."

4.331–61

She had spoken. That one was holding [his] eyes unmoved on account of the warnings of Jupiter, and having struggled, was pressing [his] concern beneath [his] heart. Finally he says a few [words]: "Queen, I shall never deny that you, who are able by speaking to list very many things, [have] deserved [very many things], nor will it displease me to remember Elissa [i.e., Dido] so long as I [am] mindful of myself, so long as breath controls these limbs. I shall say a few things on behalf of [my] case. I neither expected—don't imagine [this]—to hide this escape by stealth, nor did I ever hold out the marriage torches of a husband or come into these agreements. If the fates permitted me to lead a life by my own authority and to calm [my] cares of my own accord, I would [dwell in] the city [of] Troy first of all and would cherish the sweet remnants of my [people], [and] the lofty walls of Priam would remain, and I would have established by [my own] hand a reborn Troy for the conquered. But now, Grynean Apollo [has ordered me to pursue] great Italy, the Lycian lots have ordered [me] to pursue Italy; this [is my] love, this is [my] homeland. If the citadel[s] of Carthage and the sight of the Libyan city detain[s] you, a Phoenician, what [source of] jealousy, then, is it for [i.e., why do you begrudge] the Teucrians to settle in the Ausonian land? It is right for us, too, to seek foreign kingdoms. The troubled image of father Anchises advises and terrifies me in sleep, as often as night covers the lands with damp shadows, as often as the fiery stars rise; [my] son Ascanius [advises] me, and the wrong done to my dear son [lit., the wrong of (his) dear head], whom I am depriving of the kingdom of Hesperia and the fated fields. In fact, now an agent of the gods, sent by Jupiter himself

(I swear [on] each head), has carried down [his] orders through the swift breezes: I myself saw the god in the clear light, entering the walls [i.e., of the house] and I drew in [his] voice with these ears. Stop inflaming me and you with your laments; I pursue Italy not of [my own] accord."

AENEID 4.659–705

4.659–705

She spoke, and having pressed her face on the bed she says, "We shall die unavenged, but let us die; thus, thus does it please [me] to go beneath the shades. May the cruel Dardanian drink in with his eyes this fire from the deep [sea], and let him carry with him the omens of our death." She had spoken, and [her] companions see her collapsed in the middle of such things by/upon the sword, and the sword foaming with blood and [blood-] spattered hands. Shouting goes to the lofty courtyards; Rumor rushes through the shaken city. The halls roar with lamentations and moaning and female shrieking, the upper air resounds with great wailings, not otherwise than if, with enemies having been let in, all Carthage or ancient Tyre were to fall, and raging flames were to roll through the roofs of men and through [the roofs] of gods. [Her] sister, half-dead, heard and, terrified, with a trembling run she rushes through the midst [of the people in the palace], disfiguring [her] face with [her] nails and [her] breasts with [her] fists, and calls on the dying one by name:

"Sister, was this that [i.e., was this what you were planning]? Were you seeking me in deceit? [Was it] this [that] this pyre of yours, this [that] the fires and altars were preparing for me? Having been forsaken, what am I to complain of first? Did you, dying, spurn your sister [as] companion? [I wish that] you had called me to these same fates, that the same grief and the same hour had carried [us] both off by the sword. Indeed, did I build [your pyre] with these hands and did I call the ancestral gods with [my] voice, so that, with you having been placed thus, I might be apart [from you], cruel one? You have destroyed yourself and me, sister, and the people and Sidonian fathers and your city. Give [her to me so that] I may wash [her] wounds with water[s] and, if any last breath wanders above [her mouth], that I may collect [it] with [my] mouth."

Having spoken thus, she had passed beyond the high steps, and cradled [her] half-dead sister in [her] bosom, having embraced [her] with a groan, and dried the black blood[s] with [her] robe. That one, having tried to raise [her] heavy eyes, falls back; the wound pierced beneath [her] breast hissed.

Lifting herself three times and having leaned on [her] forearm, she raised [herself]; three times she was rolled over on the bed and with wandering eyes sought light in the high heaven and groaned, [light] having been found.

Then all-powerful Juno, having taken pity on [her] lengthy grief and difficult passing[s], sent Iris down from Olympus, to [lit., who would] release the struggling soul and the bound limbs. For since she was dying neither by fate nor by a deserved death, but pitiful[ly] before [her] time and inflamed by sudden passion, Proserpina had not yet taken a blond [lock of] hair from that one's head and had [not yet] doomed [her] [lit., the head (of the person)] to Stygian Orcus. Therefore, Iris, dewy with saffron feathers [and] drawing a thousand various colors through the sky, with the sun facing [her], flies down and stood above [Dido's] head. "Having been ordered [to do so], I take this sacred [lock of hair] for Dis [i.e., Pluto] and I release you from this body of yours": thus she speaks, and she cuts the lock with [her] right [hand], and at the same time all the heat departed and life withdrew into the winds.

Book 6
AENEID 6.295–332

6.295–304

From here [is] the way which carries [them] to the waves of Tartarean Acheron. Here, a whirlpool, wild with mud and with a vast abyss, seethes, and belches forth all the sand to Cocytus. The ferryman Charon, dreadful in [his] terrible filth, tends these waters and streams, on whose chin very much unkempt gray hair lies [lit., to whom on the chin very much unkempt grayness lies], whose [lit., to whom] eyes stand with fire [i.e., are fixed with a fiery look], [and] a filthy cloak hangs from [his] shoulders with a knot. He himself compels a boat with a pike and controls [it] with sails, and transports bodies in a rusty skiff, now an old man, but the god's old age [lit., the old age to the god] is fresh and vigorous.

6.305–16

To here rushed the whole crowd, having been poured forth to the banks, both mothers and men and bodies of great-souled heroes finished with life, boys and unwed girls, and youths placed on the funeral pyres before the faces of [their] parents: as many as the leaves that, having slipped down, fall in the woods at the first chill of autumn, or as many as the birds that are gathered at the shore from a deep whirlpool, when the cold season puts [them] to flight across the sea and sends [them] to sunny lands. They stood praying [to be] first to cross the course, and held out their hands on account of their love for the farther shore. But the gloomy boatman takes on now these, now those, but others, removed far back from the sand, he keeps off.

6.317–32

Now Aeneas, marveling and moved by the tumult, says, "O maiden, tell [me], what does this gathering at the stream want? Or what do the souls seek? Or by what distinction do these [souls] leave the shores, [while] those sweep over the dark shallows with oars?" To him the aged priestess spoke briefly thus: "[O you] sprung from Anchises, most sure offspring of the gods, you see the deep pools of Cocytus and the Stygian swamps, [by] the divine power of which the gods fear to take an oath and to deceive [i.e., the gods fear to deceive when they have taken an oath in the name of Styx]. This whole crowd which you see is poor and unburied; that [is] the ferryman Charon; these whom the wave carries [are those who have been] buried. It is not given [i.e., permitted] to transport [them] across the dread shores and sounding streams before [their] bones have rested in [their] places. They wander a hundred years and flit about these shores; finally admitted, they see again the longed-for pools." He, sprung from Anchises, stood still and [sup]pressed [his] steps, thinking many things and having pitied [their] unfair fate in [his] mind.

AENEID 6.384–425

6.384–97

They therefore continue the course undertaken and approach the river. As he looked at them [lit., whom] from the Stygian wave going through the silent grove and turning [their] foot[steps] to the bank, the boatman first addresses [them] thus with words and further reproves [them]: "Whoever you are who head toward our rivers under arms [lit., armed], come now, say why you come, and hold your step now from there where you are. This is the place of shades, of sleep, and of night made drowsy; it is not permitted [lit., unspeakable] to carry living bodies in the Stygian boat. Nor indeed did I rejoice that I had received on the lake Hercules, descendant of Alceus [lit., Alcides], as he was going, nor [did I rejoice that I had received] Theseus and Pirithoüs, although they were born from gods and undefeated in strength. That one [i.e., Hercules] sought [to put] the Tartarean guard [i.e., Cerberus] into chains and dragged [Cerberus], trembling, from the throne of the king himself; these [i.e., Theseus and Pirithoüs] attempted to abduct the queen of Dis [i.e., Proserpina] from the bedchamber."

6.398–410

The Amphrysian prophet spoke these [lit., which] things briefly in return: "No such plots [are] here (cease to be moved), nor do the weapons bring violence: let [lit., it is permitted that] the huge doorkeeper, barking eternally in [his] cave, terrify the bloodless shades, let [lit., it is permitted that] chaste Proserpina protect [her] paternal uncle's threshold. Trojan Aeneas, outstanding because of devotion to duty and arms, descends to the deep shades of Erebus to [see his] father. If no image of such great devotion moves you, nonetheless this bough" (she reveals the bough which lay hidden in [her] robe) "you should recognize." Then his heart[s], swollen from anger, settle[s] down; nor [do they say] more things than these. That one, marveling at the awe-inspiring gift of the fateful twig seen after a long time, turns [his] dark ship and approaches the shore.

6.411–25

He thereupon dislodges the other souls that had been sitting along long ridges [i.e., the benches in the boat], and releases [or clears] the gangway[s]; immediately he receives huge Aeneas in the hull [of the boat]. The sewn-together skiff groaned beneath the weight and, full of leaks, took on much swamp [i.e., water]. Finally across the river he disembarks both prophetess and man, unharmed, in the shapeless mire and grayish-green marsh grass. Huge Cerberus, lying, massive, in the facing cave, makes these realms resound with three-throated barking. The prophetess, seeing that [his] neck[s] now bristle with snakes, presents to him [lit., whom] a cake made drowsy with honey and drugged fruits. That one, laying open [his] three gullets because of ravenous hunger, snatches the offered [cake], and, poured out on the ground, relaxes his vast back[s] and is spread out, huge, in the entire cave. With its guardian buried [i.e., in sleep], Aeneas takes possession of the entrance and swift[ly] escapes the bank[s] of the irretraceable wave.

Aeneid 6.450–76

6.450–76

Among these [women] [lit., among whom] was wandering the Phoenician Dido, fresh from [her] wounding, in the great wood; as the Trojan hero first stood near her [lit., whom] and recognized [her] dim[ly] through the shadows, makes the seas resound with a hollow conch shell, foolish, and he calls the like the moon a person sees, or thinks he has seen, rising through the clouds at the beginning of the month, he released tears and addressed [her] with sweet love:

"Unhappy Dido, true, then, [was] the message [which] had come to me that [you] had been destroyed and had pursued the ultimate things [i.e., death] by means of a sword? Was I, alas, the cause of death to you? I swear by the stars, by the ones above and if there is any trustworthiness beneath the deep earth, unwilling[ly], queen, I departed from your shore. But the commands of the gods, which now compel [me] to go through these shades, through places rough with neglect and the deep night, drove [me] with their orders; nor was I able to believe that I was bringing this so great grief to you by [my] departure. Stay your step and do not withdraw yourself from our [i.e., my] gaze. Whom do you flee? This is the last [word] which, by/because of fate, I address to you."

Aeneas was attempting with such words to soothe [her] mind, burning and watching [him] grimly, and was stirring up tears. That one, turned away, was holding her eyes fixed on the ground, and is not moved in expression more by the conversation begun than if hard flint or Marpesian rock stood [there]. Finally she took herself off and, hostile, fled back into the shade bearing grove, where [her] former husband Sychaeus responds to that one in cares and matches [his] love [i.e., to hers]. Aeneas, nonetheless, struck by [her] harsh misfortune, pursues [her] with tears from afar and pities [her] going [i.e., as she goes].

AENEID 6.847–99

6.847–99

"Others will hammer out more gently breathing bronzes [i.e., sculptures]—I believe so, truly—will draw living expressions from marble, will plead cases better, and will map [better] with the compass the movements of the heavens and will tell of the rising stars [i.e., constellations]; you, Roman, remember to rule the nations with authority (these will be your arts), and to impose rule on peace, to spare the vanquished and to bring down the proud in war."

So [spoke] father Anchises, and he adds these [words] for the ones marvelling: "Look how Marcellus proceeds, outstanding with the spolia opima [i.e., a technical term for a certain category of spoils], and how [as] victor he surpasses all men. This man of equestrian rank will steady the Roman state when the great crowd is disturbing [it] [lit., the great crowd being in an uproar], will lay low the Phoenicians [i.e., Carthaginians] and the insurgent Gaul, and will hang up for Father Quirinus the third [set of] weapons won."

And here Aeneas [said] (for he saw going along a young man outstanding in beauty and with shining weapons, but [whose] brow [was] too little cheerful and eyes of/in a gloomy expression): "Who, father, [is] that one, who thus accompanies the man going [i.e., as he goes]? A son, or someone from the great lineage of descendants? What an uproar of companions about! What great impressiveness [or presence] in the man himself! But black night flies about [his] head with a sorrowful shade."

Then father Anchises, tears having sprung up, began: "O son, do not enquire into the great grief of your people; the fates will only show this man to the earth, and will not permit [him] to exist further. The Roman stock [would have] seemed too powerful to you, [gods] above, if these gifts had been secure. How many groans of men will that field [of Mars] bring to the great city of Mars! Or what funerals/deaths will you see, Tiber, when you [will] glide by the fresh[ly-made] burial mound! Neither will any boy from the Ilian [i.e., Trojan] people raise up [his] grandfathers so high [lit., into so much] with [his] promise, nor will the land of Romulus ever vaunt itself so much in any child [it has nursed]. Alas! [what] loyalty, alas! [what] old-fashioned trustworthiness, and right [hand] unvanquished in war! No one would have gone up against that one with impunity, face-to-face against him armed, either when he went as a foot soldier against the enemy or dug the sides of a foaming horse with spurs. Alas, boy to be pitied! If you were in any way to break the harsh fates—! You will [i.e., must] be Marcellus. With full hands, give lilies for me to [or let me] sprinkle purple flowers and heap up the soul of the descendant with these gifts at least, and let me perform the empty ritual." So they roam here and there in the whole region, in the broad fields of mist, and survey everything. After Anchises conducted his son through each and every one of these [lit., which] things and inflamed [his] mind with a love of the coming fame, thereupon he recalls the wars which must be waged next by the man, and he explains [about] the Laurentian peoples and the city of Latinus, and in what way he must avoid or endure [lit., both avoid and endure] each burden.

There are twin doors of Sleep, one of which is said [to be] of horn, by which an easy exit is given to true shades, the other, shining, [is] made from gleaming ivory, but the souls of the dead send false dreams to the heavens. With these words then Anchises there escorts [his] son and the Sibyl together, and sends [them] out by the ivory gate, [and] that one [i.e., Aeneas] cuts a path to the ships and sees [his] comrades again.

– Questions for Discussion and Analysis –

Based on Selected Readings from the Aeneid

I have assembled below a series of questions on the Latin passages in the accompanying textbook. My purpose has been twofold: to provide teachers with a point of departure for class lectures and discussions; and to help students prepare to be tested in essay format on their comprehension and interpretation of the texts under consideration. It should be obvious to all who consult this list that I have by no means exhausted the store of possible questions that could be raised; my goal has been far more modest: to alert readers of Vergil to the sorts of issues and questions that can help all readers begin to understand his complex poem.

To make consultation of this list of questions as convenient as possible, I have keyed each question to the relevant section of Latin text as subdivided in the accompanying textbook. In some cases, I have included questions that not only look to the selections in this textbook, but also use other episodes in the *Aeneid* as part of their frame of reference. When teachers and students are not acquainted with these other episodes, I urge them to rephrase the question to make it usable for their purposes; but I also hope hereby to remind my readers that the selections treated here are only part of a much greater poem, and that familiarity with the events, themes, and characters of the poem as a whole is fundamental to an informed comprehension of its parts.

Aeneid Book 1

1.1–7

1. How do the first three words of Book 1 establish the theme of the *Aeneid* as a whole?

2. In lines 1–3 (*Troiae . . . litora*), Vergil's style is marked by hyperbaton, i.e., the marked separation of words which belong together syntactically. What is the effect of this figure of speech here, and how does it enhance the meaning of these lines?

3. In the first seven lines of Book 1, Vergil summarizes Aeneas' journey from Troy to Italy. How do Vergil's word choice, word placement, and use of figures of speech reflect the significance and difficulty of Aeneas' journey?

1.8–11

4. In lines 8–11, Vergil asks the Muse to help him explain the divine wrath that drives Aeneas on. Identify three different Latin words or phrases used by Vergil to characterize this wrath.

5. In line 10, Vergil describes Aeneas as a man of *pietas* for the first of many times in the *Aeneid*. How is this characterization of Aeneas borne out by his behavior in Book 1—or is it?

6. In line 11 (*Tantaene . . . irae*), Vergil uses a rhetorical question to conclude his invocation of the Muse. How does this question anticipate the story told in the rest of the poem? Is this question a satisfactory summary of the poem as a whole? Make your case by referring in detail to at least three different episodes in the poem in which the gods' wrath can be seen to play a major role.

1.12–33

7. Identify three distinct features of Carthage as described by Vergil in lines 12–14 (*Urbs . . . belli*).

8. In lines 15–18 (*quam . . . fovetque*), Vergil describes Juno's fondness for Carthage. List three features characterizing her affection. How do they complement the description provided earlier in lines 12–14?

9. In line 23, Vergil uses the epithet *Saturnia* to identify and to characterize Juno. To what or to whom does this epithet refer? What reason(s) can you suggest to explain Vergil's use of it here?

10. In lines 24–28 (*prima... honores*), Vergil lists several reasons for Juno's hatred of Troy. Identify at least three of these, citing the Latin words and phrases to support your answer.

11. In line 32, Vergil mentions fate/the fates for the third time since the poem's opening (the earlier references are in lines 2 and 18). Why do you think that Vergil gives this motif such prominence in the opening lines of the *Aeneid*?

12. In line 33, Vergil concludes his summary of the story told in the *Aeneid*. How can this line be seen as a summary of the entire poem? And how does this summary complement that already provided in line 11 above?

1.34–49

13. At line 34, Vergil focuses in on the Trojans as they sail in the western Mediterranean sea towards Italy. He thus starts the story *in medias res*, an effective strategy for creating tension and excitement. How has the introduction (1–33) paved the way for the first episode? And how does Vergil create tension and excitement in this episode's opening lines (34–36)?

14. Why does Vergil describe Juno's anger as *aeternum vulnus* (36)?

15. How do the opening words of Juno's monologue (*"Mene... fatis,"* 37–39) contribute to Vergil's characterization of the goddess?

16. In lines 39–48 (*"Quippe...gero"*), Juno compares her own inability to exact revenge with Minerva's punishment of Ajax. Are the two situations really comparable? Use the text to support your point of view.

17. In lines 46–47 (*"quae ... coniunx"*) Juno explains why she feels she deserves respect. What are three of her reasons?

18. Juno ends her speech with a rhetorical question (48–49). What is the implicit answer to her question?

1.50–80

19. In lines 51–57 (*nimborum... iras*), Vergil describes the kingdom of the wind god Aeolus. Identify three figures of speech or rhetorical devices *other than* alliteration/assonance that Vergil uses to enhance the vividness of these lines.

20. How do lines 51–63 characterize Aeolus himself? Is he an absolute monarch, or is his power limited in any way?

21. In lines 69–70 (*"incute ... ponto"*), Juno suggests four ways Aeolus can damage Aeneas' fleet. What are they?

22. Juno offers Aeolus marriage to the nymph Deiopea in return for his help with disturbing Aeneas' ships (72–75). How does Juno ensure the success of her offer?

23. In lines 76–80 (*"Tuus ... potentem"*), Aeolus describes Juno's power in the universe generally and over him in particular. Do you think that his response would please Juno? Give three reasons for your explanation.

24. What is the purpose of Aeolus' emphatic repetition of the word *tu* in lines 78–79?

1.81–123

25. In lines 81–91, Vergil describes the storm created by Aeolus. How does the structure of Vergil's narrative reflect the destructiveness of the storm?

26. In lines 92–94 (*Extemplo ... refert*), Aeneas himself is introduced as a character in the poem and in the storm created by Aeolus. What first impression of his character do these lines create?

27. In lines 94–101 (*"O ... volvit"*), Aeneas laments the fact that he did not die along with the other great Trojan heroes at Troy. In particular, he mentions Hector and Sarpedon, both of whom will be alluded to again in the *Aeneid*. Were the fates of these two men in fact enviable? You may wish to look at the scenes in the *Iliad* in which the deaths of these two heroes are depicted to support your discussion with specific details.

28. Aeneas' first speech in the *Aeneid* (94–101) has sometimes been criticized for its mournful tone, but has also been considered profoundly moving. Do you think that this speech contributes to a positive or negative first impression of our hero?

29. In line 95, Aeneas refers to the good fortune of those Trojans who died at home and in the sight of their parents (*"ante ora patrum Troiae sub moenibus altis"*). What factor(s) relating to the context for this speech help to make this reference particularly poignant here?

30. In lines 102–117, Vergil returns to a detailed description of the storm and its destructive powers. Locate four figures of speech and rhetorical devices used in this passage that contribute to the violence of the description.

31. Readers have frequently commented on the visual nature of this description (102–17), and have compared it to painted or even filmed narrative. Draw a picture of or otherwise illustrate Vergil's storm in a visual medium. In your opinion, which medium allows for greater detail, the verbal or the visual? Why?

32. In lines 118–19 (*Apparent . . . undas*), Vergil offers a brief description of the storm's aftermath. How does the arrangement of words in these lines complement their meaning?

33. In line 119, Vergil echoes the opening words of Book 1 (*arma virum*). What is the effect of this echo?

34. In lines 120–23, Vergil closes the storm scene by focusing in on the damage done to the Trojan ships. How much damage has in fact been done to Aeneas' fleet? How many ships have been destroyed?

1.124–56

35. In lines 124–27, Neptune emerges from the sea and into the poem, so to speak. Define and describe four figures of speech or rhetorical devices used by Vergil to mark the importance of this entrance. What first impression of Neptune is Vergil seeking to achieve?

36. We have already seen in the storm scene the imbalance of power between Juno and Aeolus, as well as its consequences. With the appearance of Neptune on the scene in line 125, the divine hierarchy is further complicated. How is Neptune related to Juno and Aeolus? And how is his relationship to them likely to affect the divine balance of power?

37. In line 130, Vergil uses the words *doli . . . Iunonis et irae* to describe Neptune's perception of the storm and its causes. Is his sense of Juno's motivation justified? What is its basis?

38. In lines 132–41 (*"Tantane . . . regnet"*), Neptune addresses the winds who have caused so much trouble for the Trojans, and reasserts his control over them. What features of structure, style, and word choice make this a particularly effective speech?

39. In line 135 (*"Quos ego—"*), we find the most famous example of aposiopesis in all of Latin literature. Can you think of any particularly striking instances of this device in English?

40. In lines 142–47 (*Sic... undas*), Vergil describes how Neptune and his attendants restore peace at sea. How does this passage reflect in its style the speed and ease with which Neptune acts?

41. In 148–53 (*Ac... mulcet*), Vergil uses the first extended simile in the *Aeneid* to describe the effect of Neptune's calming powers on the chaos around him. How do the features of the simile correspond to details in the storm narrative?

42. In this simile, Vergil describes a man of outstanding *pietas* (151) who by the power of his presence is able to calm those around him. While it is clear that Vergil intends in the first place to compare Neptune with this man, his use of the word *pietas* also makes it likely that he means us to think of Aeneas himself. Why might Vergil wish us to see Neptune and Aeneas as similar?

43. With lines 154–56, Vergil closes the storm scene. How do these lines provide an effective ending for this episode, and a transition to the next?

1.157–209

44. With the ecphrasis of the cave of the Nymphs in lines 159–69, Vergil again presents his reader with a striking example of visual narrative. Identify five figures of speech/rhetorical devices Vergil uses to create this vivid picture.

45. The cave of the Nymphs is perceived by the Trojans as a safe harbor where they may rest and recover from the effects of the storm. Is their perception accurate? How does Vergil make the cave seem inviting and safe? And is it so in fact?

46. In lines 170–79 (*Huc... saxo*), Vergil describes in detail the landing of the Trojans on the Libyan shore and their first actions there. How does Vergil use the contrast between wet and dry states to emphasize this transition?

47. In lines 180–94 (*Aeneas... omnes*), Vergil depicts Aeneas' first actions upon arriving on the Libyan shore. How does this scene contribute to our evaluation of Aeneas' abilities as a leader?

48. In line 197, Vergil describes Aeneas as soothing his men with his words (*dictis ... mulcet*). This expression has already been used once in Book 1—where? And what parallel does this repetition suggest?

49. In lines 198–207, Aeneas delivers his second speech in the *Aeneid* (the first appears at lines 94–102). Compare the contents of the two speeches as well as their respective audiences. How does the second speech modify your evaluation of Aeneas' character? Or does it?

50. Evaluate the effectiveness of Aeneas' speech. If you were one of his men, would you be reassured? Why?

51. In lines 208–9 (*Talia ... dolorem*), Vergil provides some insight into Aeneas' thoughts. Does this insight have any effect on your evaluation of the preceding speech? Why?

1.418–40

52. As Aeneas and Achates approach Carthage, they are awed by what they see (lines 418–22). Identify at least four remarkable features of the new city as described here by Vergil.

53. In lines 423–29 (*Instant ... futuris*), Vergil gives a vivid description of the various activities in which the Carthaginians are engaged. Identify at least eight of these activities, and consider the sequence in which Vergil lists them: what does the arrangement suggest about the relative importance of each of these activities?

54. In lines 430–36 (*Qualis ... mella*), Vergil uses a simile comparing the Carthaginian laborers to bees, and notes several of the activities in which bees are typically engaged. How effective is the parallel suggested by this simile? Can you detect any differences between the way in which Vergil describes the Carthaginians and the way in which he describes the bees?

55. Walls (*moenia*, 437) are an important symbol in Roman tradition (and in classical thought generally) of stability, permanence, and civilization; they are also useful for the exclusion of foreigners and defense against enemies. Which of these meanings do the Carthaginian walls have for Aeneas? And which of these meanings do the Carthaginian walls have for the Carthaginians themselves?

1.494–519

56. The arrival of Dido on the scene in lines 494–97 (*Haec . . . caterva*) brings the ecphrasis to an abrupt end. Does Vergil give any indication that the last scene he describes (lines 491–93) is in fact the last scene on the temple, or is Aeneas poised to look further?

57. In lines 498–502, Vergil compares Dido to the goddess Diana. A Diana look-alike has already appeared once in Book 1—where? And what does the repetition of imagery associated with Diana suggest about Dido?

58. Vergil's simile here is modeled on a Homeric simile, used to describe Odysseus' reaction when he first sees the princess Nausicaa on Phaeacia after he has been washed ashore there. Read this episode in *Odyssey* Book 6, and compare Vergil's simile to Homer's. How is Vergil's different? And why might Vergil have wanted to introduce such variations?

59. Scenes involving hunting and hunting imagery appear repeatedly in Book 1. Identify three episodes seen so far in which hunting or hunting imagery plays a major role, and discuss the effect of Vergil's repeated use of this motif.

60. In her earlier description of queen Dido, Venus had used the phrase "*dux femina facti*" (364). How does Dido's leadership manifest itself in this scene as Aeneas watches her? Identify three distinct features in the description of Dido in lines 494–519 that support Venus' description.

1.520–60

61. Aeneas' companion Ilioneus delivers a lengthy speech to Dido requesting her assistance. Considering the speech as a whole (522–60), assess its effectiveness. What makes Ilioneus persuasive?

62. The first sentence of Ilioneus' speech (522–26) characterizes the relationship of the Trojans to Dido. Write out and translate three words or phrases in this passage that contribute to this characterization.

63. Ilioneus' first words to Dido associate her and Carthage with Jupiter. What is the basis for making this connection? Can you recall any earlier mention of this in Book 1?

64. Ilioneus devotes six lines to a depiction of the Trojans' current pitiable condition (524–29). Identify four words or phrases in these lines calculated to arouse Dido's sympathy. How do they do so?

65. Ilioneus' description of their destination, Hesperia, focuses on the land and its people (530–34). How does he characterize them? Is this characterization consistent with earlier mentions of Hesperia in Book 1?

66. Ilioneus' description of the storm that brought them to Carthage is brief but vivid (535–38). Identify at least four features of the storm highlighted by Ilioneus.

67. Ilioneus questions the behavior of the people they met on the shores of Carthage (539–41). Why do you think Vergil has not described these events elsewhere in his narrative?

68. Ilioneus' first mention of Aeneas (544–45) is highly laudatory. What does this tell you about the Trojans' view of their leader? Do you think Ilioneus is sincere? Why?

69. Ilioneus next wants to reassure Dido that, if she helps them, she won't regret it (546–50). How does he do so? Is his argument persuasive?

70. The imagery Ilioneus uses to express his hope that Aeneas is still alive is unusual: *"si vescitur aura aetheria"* (546–47). Why do you think he uses this expression?

71. Who is Acestes (550)? Why does Ilioneus mention him here?

72. In 551–52, Ilioneus mentions three things he and his men must do to repair the fleet. What are they? Write out and translate the Latin phrases that support your response.

73. In 553–54, Ilioneus names the Trojans' hoped-for destination three times. What is the effect of this repetition? What other words in these lines can support your interpretation?

74. Ilioneus closes his speech with a description of the Trojans' back-up plan (555–58). What is it? Does it make sense?

1.561–78

75. Dido responds to Ilioneus and the other Trojans by trying to reassure them. Considering her speech as a whole (562–78), assess its effectiveness. Does she respond to everything in Ilioneus' speech?

76. Identify three things Dido says or does in 561–62 that are meant to reassure the Trojans.

77. Dido gives two reasons for the security measures she has taken to protect Carthage (563–64). What are they? And how do they contribute to her characterization?

78. At 565–68, Dido tells the Trojans that their recent history is well known in Carthage. Is she convincing? Support your answer with reference to specific words and phrases in the passage.

79. We have already learned in an earlier passage of Book 1 that the Carthaginians know about the Trojan War. Where do we learn this? Is the description of the war in that earlier passage consistent with what Dido says here?

80. At 569–71, Dido promises to help the Trojans no matter where they choose to go. How many possible destinations does she mention? Are these identical to the ones mentioned by Ilioneus, or not?

81. In 569–70, Dido refers to Italy as "*Saturnia . . . arva*" and to Sicily as "*Erycis fines.*" Where do you think she has learned these names? And what does her knowledge tell you about her?

82. At 572–74, Dido mentions a third alternative: she invites the Trojans to settle with her people in Carthage. What do you think of this offer—is it realistic? And what does this offer tell you about Dido's leadership abilities?

83. Dido closes her speech (575–78) with a wish that Aeneas himself were present, and promises to send out search parties to find him. In what locations does she promise to search? Write out and translate at least three different words or phrases she uses to identify these locales.

84. How would you characterize Dido's wish that Aeneas himself were present (575–76)? Is it sympathetic, overly emotional, foreboding, or simply realistic? And is this impression consistent with what you have already learned about Dido in Book 1?

AENEID *Book 2*

2.40–56

1. One of the first words used by Aeneas to describe the priest Laocoon is *ardens* (41). What is its meaning here?

2. In lines 42–49 (*'O...ferentes'*) Laocoon addresses the people of Troy. Is this a rhetorically compelling speech? Support your answer with reference to the text.

3. In lines 50–53 (*"Sic...cavernae"*), Aeneas describes the hurling of Laocoon's spear and its impact. Identify three figures of speech/rhetorical devices used by Aeneas to make this a particularly vivid and emotional description.

4. In lines 54–56, Aeneas uses a so-called mixed condition, combining both tenses of the subjunctive (imperfect and pluperfect) used in contrary-to-fact conditions as well as the pluperfect indicative *impulerat*. Explain the logic underlying Aeneas' choice of tenses and moods here.

2.201–227

5. In lines 203–4, Vergil separates the epithet *gemini* far apart from the word it modifies, *angues*. What is the effect of this separation (hyperbaton) on Aeneas' audience?

6. In line 209, the clause *"Fit sonitus spumante salo"* is virtually impersonal, i.e., no hearer is specified. What effect does this sort of description have on its audience? And how do other features of these words enhance this effect?

7. Aeneas focuses particular attention in his description of the snakes on how their eyes look, i.e., *"ardentes...oculos suffecti sanguine et igni"* (210). How literally are we to take this description? Support your answer with reference to the text.

8. Aeneas describes the movement of the snakes toward Laocoon with a military metaphor, *"agmine certo"* (212). Why do you think Aeneas uses this metaphor?

9. The description of the snakes' assault in lines 213–19 (*"et ... altis"*) uses language associated with several of the five senses (i.e., sight, taste, smell, hearing, and touch). Find an example in this passage of at least one word or phrase associated with three of these senses, and describe the effect of this appeal to the senses on Aeneas' audience.

10. The scene of the snakes' attack on Laocoon and his sons as described by Aeneas is often compared to the famous Laocoon sculpture depicted on p. 50. Which representation of the story do you prefer, and why?

11. Do you think that Vergil was familiar with the Laocoon sculpture when he composed this scene? Use Vergil's text as the basis for your argument.

12. What is the rhetorical purpose of Aeneas' uses of tmesis, or the cutting of one word into two parts (*"circum ... dati"*), in lines 218–19?

13. In lines 223–24 (*"qualis ... securim"*), Aeneas uses a simile to compare the bellowing of Laocoon to that of a bull in the process of being slaughtered. Why do you think Aeneas chooses to use this simile in particular, i.e., what does it tell us about Laocoon and his suffering?

14. After wreaking their destruction the snakes depart swiftly and smoothly (lines 225–27). Why do you think Vergil focuses on the nature of their departure to end this scene?

2.228–49

15. In lines 228–33 (*"Tum ... conclamant"*), Aeneas offers an ironic summary of the effect of Laocoon's suffering upon the other Trojans. Identify at least three ironic details in this passage.

16. Some scholars think that lines like 235 here are incomplete because Vergil did not finish the *Aeneid* before he died. Can you think of any other explanation for the incomplete line that is relevant to the story Aeneas is telling?

17. In lines 234–40 (*"Dividimus ... urbi"*), Aeneas describes the actions taken by the Trojans as they receive the horse into the city. Identify three separate actions mentioned by Aeneas here.

18. How difficult must it have been to move the horse into the city? Use the description given in lines 234–40 to support your answer.

19. Identify three figures of speech/rhetorical devices used by Aeneas in lines 241–42 (*"O ... Dardanidum"*) to communicate his strong emotion.

20. In line 245, Aeneas refers to the horse as a *"monstrum infelix."* How do the etymologies of both of these words (*monstrum* from *moneo*, 'warn,' and *infelix* from *fero*, 'bear' or 'be fertile') help to explain Aeneas' choice of words?

2.268–97

21. In line 269, Aeneas describes sleep as a gift of the gods (*"dono divum"*). Given what we have already learned about gifts in Book 2, what are the implications of this expression here?

22. In lines 270–73, Aeneas describes the appearance of Hector at the time of his death. How did Hector die?

23. In lines 274–76, Aeneas recalls two of Hector's greatest accomplishments as described in the *Iliad*. What are they?

24. In describing the conversation he had with Hector in his dream, Aeneas uses the verb *videbar* of himself (line 279). Why? What is the effect of this verb here?

25. In lines 281–86, Aeneas quotes the speech he delivered to Hector's ghost in his sleep. What figures of speech/rhetorical devices does he use in this speech to express his emotional state?

26. Hector's response in lines 289–95 (*"Heu … ponto"*) is straightforward and clear. Identify at least four things Hector tells Aeneas to do.

27. Throughout this scene, Vergil has used language relating to hiding and concealment to describe the fall of Troy. Identify at least five different words Vergil uses that are in some way associated with this motif. What is the effect of the repetition of this motif on Vergil's reader?

2.559–587

28. After the death of Priam, Aeneas is suddenly reminded of his own father, his home, and his family (559–66). Vergil thus uses the father-son theme as a link to the next scene; how do Aeneas' thoughts of his home, wife, and son also support this link?

29. In line 560, Aeneas describes his sudden recollection of his father as the apparition of an *imago*, a word often used to describe the appearance of a dead person in one's dreams. Is Aeneas' father already dead? How can you tell?

30. As he recalls his first view of Helen in the ruins of Troy, Aeneas emphasizes the sense of sight (567–70). Write out all of the words and phrases in this passage that refer to the sense of sight; are any other senses evoked at any point in the passage?

31. Aeneas mentions that Helen is staying near the temple of Vesta ("*limina Vestae servantem*," 567–68). Who is the goddess Vesta, and what do you know about her? Does she appear elsewhere in the *Aeneid*? And why do you think that Helen might seek safety in Vesta's temple?

32. In 571–73, Aeneas identifies three persons or things that Helen is afraid of. What are these three entities? Write out and translate the words or phrases for each of the three.

33. In 571–76, Aeneas explains the reasons motivating Helen to conceal herself, and describes his own negative feelings about her. Identify at least three figures of speech or rhetorical devices that he uses to emphasize his feelings. How would you describe their effect here?

34. In 577–87, Aeneas expresses what must have originally been an internal monologue, in which he asks himself sarcastically whether Helen should be allowed to escape without punishment or will indeed be forced to pay for the destruction she has caused Troy, and encourages himself to play the role of avenger. How is this monologue structured? Do you think it is a realistic representation of an internal debate? Use words and phrases drawn from the text to support your answer.

35. In 580, Aeneas considers that Helen is likely to go home to Greece in the company of Trojan women and attendants ("*Iliadum turba et Phrygiis comitata ministris*"). Why does he think this? And how does your understanding of this line contribute to your approval (or disapproval) of Aeneas' wrath?

2.588–620

36. In 589–93, Aeneas describes a meeting with his mother Venus. This is not his first meeting with her in the poem (i.e., not first in the sequence of the narrative as we read the poem); she also appears to him at 1.314–417. Compare the two passages, considering both the specific language Vergil uses and the way Venus interacts with her son in each. How would you explain the difference between the two scenes?

37. The appearance of Venus to her son in 589–92 is strikingly different from the appearance of Helen Aeneas describes moments before, in 567–74. Compare these two visions; how do the differences set up a contrast between the two female characters described? And what do the different descriptions tell us about Aeneas' feelings about them?

38. The remainder of this passage (594–620) consists of an address by Venus to her son. Considering the speech as a whole, identify at least three major points Venus makes in her attempt to convince Aeneas to take action. Do you consider her speech to be rhetorically persuasive? Why?

39. In 594–600, Venus expresses her concern for those closest to Aeneas. Whom does she mention? And what does she think has happened to them?

40. In 601–18, Venus dissuades Aeneas from taking vengeance by assuring him that the gods will do so. How many gods does she single out in particular? Explain why each of these gods bears a special grudge against Troy and its people.

41. While she speaks, Venus removes the cloud that had been obscuring Aeneas' view of his surroundings (604–7). What are her reasons for doing so? Use the events described in this episode to support your answer.

42. At the close of her speech (619–20), Venus promises to help her son. Identify two ways she intends to do so; from what you know of the rest of the poem, does she in fact live up to her promises?

AENEID *Book 4*

4.160–218

1. The description of the storm in lines 160–68 is extremely ominous. What figures of speech/rhetorical devices does Vergil use here to increase our sense of foreboding as we read?

2. How sympathetic is Vergil to Dido? Use his comments in lines 169–72 as the basis for your answer.

3. Vergil's description of Fama (lines 173–88) creates a terrifying personification of an abstract force. Besides personification, what figures of speech/rhetorical devices does Vergil use to explain Fama's power?

4. Scan line 181. How does the metrical pattern of the line complement its meaning?

5. In line 188, Vergil indicates that Fama reports both true and false rumors. Is there anything untrue about the rumors she spreads in lines 191–94?

6. Compare the ritual activities of Iarbas here (lines 198–202) with those of Dido in lines 56–64. How similar are their goals?

7. Iarbas' speech to Jupiter betrays his wounded pride, much as Juno's speech had betrayed hers in Book 1.37–49. Compare these two speeches: what structural features and rhetorical devices do they have in common?

8. In lines 215–17, Iarbas uses several cultural stereotypes to insult Aeneas and his men. Does Vergil provide any indication in the remainder of the *Aeneid* that these stereotypes may have a basis in truth?

4.259–95

9. In lines 260–64, Vergil describes Aeneas as Mercury sees him when he arrives in Carthage. What are we supposed to think of Aeneas' appearance? And how does his appearance complement the activities in which he is engaged?

10. In lines 265–76 (*"Tu … debetur"*), Mercury addresses Aeneas and gives him Jupiter's message. How closely does Mercury's speech represent what Jupiter had told him to say? And how similar is the tone of Mercury's speech to that of Jupiter?

11. Vergil describes Aeneas' reaction to Mercury's speech as a combination of shock and terror (279–80). What features of Mercury's speech and presentation are likely to have added to Aeneas' dread?

12. In lines 281–86, Vergil vividly depicts Aeneas' inner turmoil. What figures of speech/rhetorical devices does Vergil use in this passage to help us understand Aeneas' emotional state of mind?

13. In lines 288–94, Vergil lists the things Aeneas decides to do. How many activities are included? List them, and discuss the effect of listing them in the order provided by Vergil.

4.296–361

14. In lines 300–303, Dido is compared to a frenzied Bacchant as she hears the rumors about Aeneas' impending departure. Does this simile arouse sympathy for her in Vergil's reader? Support your response with reference to the Latin text.

15. In her speech to Aeneas (305–30), Dido moves from anger to sarcasm, from reproach to desperation. Discuss the range of emotions reflected in her speech, and evaluate the speech's general persuasiveness.

16. In lines 307–8, Dido speaks of herself in the third person. What is the intended effect of this rhetorical device?

17. In lines 320–26, Dido mentions a number of political reasons for her not to want to lose Aeneas. Some of the same reasons have been used elsewhere in Book 4 to convince Dido that a marriage to Aeneas would be advantageous. Where are these earlier discussions of political expedience? And are they consistent with what Dido says here?

18. Dido's wish for a *"parvulus . . . Aeneas"* (328–29) evokes the theme of the role of children in the continuity of the family and the survival of the Trojans. Where else has this theme been developed in Book 4, and by whom?

19. In lines 336–61, Aeneas defends himself to Dido. Is this a convincing speech of self-defense? Does it allow us to feel sympathy for Aeneas' point of view? Use specific features of Aeneas' speech to make your case.

4.659–705

20. Fama appears for the last time in Book 4 at line 666. Consider how her presence permeates Book 4, discussing at least three different scenes in which Fama/fama is featured. Why is she of such great thematic significance in this book and in the *Aeneid* generally?

21. In lines 675–85 (*"Hoc ... legam"*), Anna expresses her astonishment at Dido's sudden suicide. Should she be surprised? Is there any way she could have anticipated Dido's intentions? Use her speech to support your discussion.

22. In lines 688–92, Vergil describes Dido's dying actions. Why does he include this scene? It would have been possible for him not to include it; what effect do you think he is striving to achieve with it?

23. Juno appears in lines 693–95, and sends down Iris to release Dido from life. Why doesn't Juno go herself? Can you think of a parallel to this use of a divine intermediary that occurs elsewhere in Book 4?

24. Dido's departure from life coincides with the end of the book. Is this a satisfying conclusion, or do important questions raised in the book remain unanswered? Use the text to support your discussion.

AENEID *Book 6*

6.295–332

1. The opening lines of this passage give us Aeneas' impressions as he approaches the river Acheron (295–97). What are these impressions? Can you tell from any details in the passage what emotions Aeneas feels as he proceeds?

2. Charon's appearance is described in detail in 298–304. Citing particular words and phrases in the passage, identify at least four different aspects of his appearance. What impression, if any, does he make on his viewers?

3. Charon is surrounded by many denizens of the underworld, eager to cross the river (305–8). How many different groups of people are included in this crowd? And how is the list organized? Does Vergil emphasize some members of the group over others, and if so, how does he do so?

4. The simile in 309–12 compares the behavior of the members of this crowd to two different natural phenomena: what are they? Do both of these comparisons work equally well, or is one better than the other? Why?

5. The simile in 309–12 contains many descriptive details that do not contribute directly to the comparison, i.e., that have little or nothing to do with groups massed in a crowd. Write out and translate the specific words or phrases for at least two of these details, and discuss how they contribute to the comparison.

6. In 313–16, Vergil devotes two lines to a description of the behavior of the crowds around Charon, and two lines to his response. What figures of speech and rhetorical devices help to enhance the balance between the two pairs of lines?

7. Aeneas asks the Sibyl to explain the behavior of this crowd (317–20). What aspects of their behavior particularly interest him? What details does he notice? And what does he not seem to notice?

8. In 321–30, the Sibyl explains that the group actually consists of two separate sections. What is the distinction between the two? And how does this distinction determine their fate in the underworld?

9. The Sibyl begins her speech with a solemn address to Aeneas (*"Anchisa generate, deum certissima proles,"* 322). How does this address reflect what she has learned about Aeneas earlier in Book 6?

10. The importance of funerary rites (burial and/or cremation) for the dead appears several times in the *Aeneid* outside of this passage (321–30). From your reading of other sections of the poem, identify at least two other characters who die and whose funeral is described in detail, and in an essay analyze the significance of these scenes for the plot.

11. Vergil closes this episode with a description of Aeneas' reaction to the Sibyl's speech (331–32). How do these lines contribute to your understanding of Aeneas' character?

6.384–425

12. As Aeneas and the Sibyl proceed, Vergil describes their location as "a silent grove" (*tacitum nemus*, 386). Why does he mention this detail? And is it consistent with the previous descriptions of the underworld in Book 6?

13. In 388–97, Charon addresses Aeneas alone, ignoring the Sibyl. Why do you think he doesn't mention her? And why is he so focused on Aeneas?

14. In his speech (388–97), Charon alludes in passing to various features of the underworld landscape. Write out and translate at least three different words or phrases he uses to describe the place.

15. In 392–97, Charon alludes to the earlier and unwelcome visits of Hercules, Theseus, and Pirithoüs to the underworld. What does he say these characters did? Is there any evidence elsewhere in the *Aeneid* to substantiate his claim? And why does he think that Aeneas is comparable to them?

16. In 397, Charon alludes to the story of the goddess Proserpina (*"dominam Ditis"*). What associations does this goddess have in ancient myth? And why does she dwell in the underworld?

17. Although Charon questions only Aeneas, the Sibyl is the one who replies (399–407). Why do you think she does so? Use what you know about the three characters involved to explain her role in this scene.

18. The Sibyl closes her speech by revealing the golden bough to Charon (406–7). Why is this object significant? Locate the passages earlier in Book 6 where it is described, and use them to explain the effect of the golden bough on Charon here.

19. When Aeneas boards Charon's boat (412–14), Vergil emphasizes the contrast between the two—he is large, but it is small. What is the point of this contrast?

20. Once Aeneas goes across the river, he still must get past Cerberus (417–23). Who or what is this creature? How is he described, and what is most threatening about him? Write out and translate the words or phrases that support your answer.

21. The episode closes with two lines describing Aeneas' escape from Cerberus (424–25). How do these lines contribute to your understanding of Aeneas' destiny?

6.450–76

22. As the word *recens* in line 450 reminds us, Dido's suicide had occurred not long before. Does Vergil provide enough information about the passage of time experienced by the Trojans in Book 5 for us to determine how long it in fact has been? You should read Book 5 in English to help you answer this question.

23. In line 455, Aeneas mentions the *"verus . . . nuntius"* that reported her death to him. How would he have received this message? And who might its bearer have been?

24. Is Aeneas' speech (lines 455–66) a compelling self-defense or not? Discuss the rhetorical strengths and weaknesses of this speech. Can you think of anything more Aeneas might have said in his own defense, or any arguments against him that Dido might have used had she chosen to speak in response?

25. Vergil uses imagery associated with darkness and light repeatedly in Book 6 to describe the events in Cumae and in the underworld. Focusing on this scene (450–76), analyze Vergil's use of this imagery. How does it contribute to the characterization of both Dido and Aeneas here?

6.847–99

26. In lines 847–50, Anchises lists the civilized accomplishments to be achieved by people other than the Romans. How many different areas of accomplishment does he mention? And what are they?

27. In line 851, Anchises uses the vocative *"Romane"* to address both Aeneas and, by extension, all of his descendants. This epithet is an anachronism. Why?

28. In lines 851–53, Anchises lists what he believes to be distinctively Roman accomplishments, or *artes*. What are they? Do you think that Vergil's readers at the end of the first century BCE would have agreed?

29. In lines 855–59, Anchises describes the elder Marcellus. What figures of speech/rhetorical devices does he use to enhance the vividness of the description? And which of Marcellus' many accomplishments does he seem to think most worthy of note?

30. In lines 863–66, Aeneas describes the younger Marcellus. List four features Aeneas notes in his description. What do these four features tell Aeneas about the young man, whom he of course cannot recognize?

31. In his response to Aeneas (lines 868–86), Anchises describes how and why the young Marcellus will be mourned. How many accomplishments of the young Marcellus does he list, and what are they?

32. What sort of funeral does Anchises envision for Marcellus? Compare this imaginary funeral to another funeral depicted in the *Aeneid*. What features do they have in common?

33. The young Marcellus is the last in a long parade of heroes in the underworld as described by Anchises to Aeneas in Book 6. What reasons might Vergil have had for putting him at the end of this parade? And what effect does this placement have on the reader?

34. In lines 888–92, Vergil summarizes the various lessons and instructions given by Anchises to Aeneas to encourage him as he pursues his goal of creating a new home for the Trojans in Italy. Find at least two references Vergil makes here to other episodes in the *Aeneid*.

35. In lines 893–99, Vergil describes the two gates from the underworld. Why do you think that Aeneas and the Sibyl depart from the underworld by means of the ivory gate?

—— Latin Text of Selections —— from Vergil's *Aeneid*

Book 1

Book 1.1–209

Arma virumque cano, Troiae qui primus ab oris

Italiam fato profugus Laviniaque venit

litora, multum ille et terris iactatus et alto

vi superum, saevae memorem Iunonis ob iram,

5 multa quoque et bello passus, dum conderet urbem

inferretque deos Latio; genus unde Latinum

Albanique patres atque altae moenia Romae.

Musa, mihi causas memora, quo numine laeso

quidve dolens regina deum tot volvere casus

10 insignem pietate virum, tot adire labores

impulerit. Tantaene animis caelestibus irae?

Urbs antiqua fuit (Tyrii tenuere coloni)

Karthago, Italiam contra Tiberinaque longe

ostia, dives opum studiisque asperrima belli,

15 quam Iuno fertur terris magis omnibus unam

posthabita coluisse Samo. hic illius arma,

hic currus fuit; hoc regnum dea gentibus esse,

si qua fata sinant, iam tum tenditque fovetque.

Progeniem sed enim Troiano a sanguine duci

20 audierat Tyrias olim quae verteret arces;

hinc populum late regem belloque superbum

venturum excidio Libyae; sic volvere Parcas.

Id metuens veterisque memor Saturnia belli,

prima quod ad Troiam pro caris gesserat Argis—

25 necdum etiam causae irarum saevique dolores

exciderant animo; manet alta mente repostum

iudicium Paridis spretaeque iniuria formae

et genus invisum et rapti Ganymedis honores:

his accensa super iactatos aequore toto

30 Troas, reliquias Danaum atque immitis Achilli,

arcebat longe Latio, multosque per annos

errabant acti fatis maria omnia circum.

Tantae molis erat Romanam condere gentem.

Vix e conspectu Siculae telluris in altum

35 vela dabant laeti et spumas salis aere ruebant,

cum Iuno aeternum servans sub pectore vulnus

haec secum: "Mene incepto desistere victam

nec posse Italia Teucrorum avertere regem!

Quippe vetor fatis. Pallasne exurere classem

40 Argivum atque ipsos potuit summergere ponto

unius ob noxam et furias Aiacis Oilei?

Ipsa Iovis rapidum iaculata e nubibus ignem

disiecitque rates evertitque aequora ventis

illum exspirantem transfixo pectore flammas

45 turbine corripuit scopuloque infixit acuto;

ast ego, quae divum incedo regina Iovisque

et soror et coniunx, una cum gente tot annos

bella gero. Et quisquam numen Iunonis adorat

praeterea aut supplex aris imponet honorem?"

50 Talia flammato secum dea corde volutans

nimborum in patriam, loca feta furentibus Austris,

Aeoliam venit. hic vasto rex Aeolus antro

luctantes ventos tempestatesque sonoras

imperio premit ac vinclis et carcere frenat.

Illi indignantes magno cum murmure montis

55 circum claustra fremunt; celsa sedet Aeolus arce

sceptra tenens mollitque animos et temperat iras.

ni faciat, maria ac terras caelumque profundum

quippe ferant rapidi secum verrantque per auras;

Sed pater omnipotens speluncis abdidit atris

60 hoc metuens molemque et montes insuper altos

imposuit, regemque dedit qui foedere certo

et premere et laxas sciret dare iussus habenas.

Ad quem tum Iuno supplex his vocibus usa est:

65 "Aeole (namque tibi divum pater atque hominum rex

et mulcere dedit fluctus et tollere vento),

gens inimica mihi Tyrrhenum navigat aequor

Ilium in Italiam portans victosque penates:

incute vim ventis submersasque obrue puppes,

70 aut age diversos et dissice corpora ponto.

Sunt mihi bis septem praestanti corpore Nymphae,

quarum quae forma pulcherrima Deiopea,

conubio iungam stabili propriamque dicabo,

omnes ut tecum meritis pro talibus annos

75 exigat et pulchra faciat te prole parentem."

Aeolus haec contra: "Tuus, O regina, quid optes

explorare labor; mihi iussa capessere fas est.

Tu mihi quodcumque hoc regni, tu sceptra Iovemque

concilias, tu das epulis accumbere divum

80   nimborumque facis tempestatumque potentem."

Haec ubi dicta, cavum conversa cuspide montem

impulit in latus; ac venti velut agmine facto,

qua data porta, ruunt et terras turbine perflant.

Incubuere mari totumque a sedibus imis

85   una Eurusque Notusque ruunt creberque procellis

Africus, et vastos volvunt ad litora fluctus.

Insequitur clamorque virum stridorque rudentum;

eripiunt subito nubes caelumque diemque

Teucrorum ex oculis; ponto nox incubat atra;

intonuere poli et crebris micat ignibus aether

90   praesentemque viris intentant omnia mortem.

Extemplo Aeneae solvuntur frigore membra;

ingemit et duplices tendens ad sidera palmas

talia voce refert: "O terque quaterque beati,

95   quis ante ora patrum Troiae sub moenibus altis

contigit oppetere! O Danaum fortissime gentis

Tydide! Mene Iliacis occumbere campis

non potuisse tuaque animam hanc effundere dextra,

saevus ubi Aeacidae telo iacet Hector, ubi ingens

100 Sarpedon, ubi tot Simois correpta sub undis

scuta virum galeasque et fortia corpora volvit!"

Talia iactanti stridens Aquilone procella

velum adversa ferit, fluctusque ad sidera tollit.

Franguntur remi, tum prora avertit et undis

105　dat latus, insequitur cumulo praeruptus aquae mons.

Hi summo in fluctu pendent; his unda dehiscens

terram inter fluctus aperit, furit aestus harenis.

Tres Notus abreptas in saxa latentia torquet

(saxa vocant Itali mediis quae in fluctibus Aras,

110　dorsum immane mari summo), tres Eurus ab alto

in brevia et syrtes urget, miserabile visu,

inliditque vadis atque aggere cingit harenae.

Unam, quae Lycios fidumque vehebat Oronten,

ipsius ante oculos ingens a vertice pontus

115　in puppim ferit: excutitur pronusque magister

volvitur in caput, ast illam ter fluctus ibidem

torquet agens circum et rapidus vorat aequore vertex.

Apparent rari nantes in gurgite vasto,

arma virum tabulaeque et Troia gaza per undas.

120　Iam validam Ilionei navem, iam fortis Achatae,

et qua vectus Abas, et qua grandaevus Aletes,

vicit hiems; laxis laterum compagibus omnes

accipiunt inimicum imbrem rimisque fatiscunt.

Interea magno misceri murmure pontum

125 emissamque hiemem sensit Neptunus et imis

stagna refusa vadis, graviter commotus, et alto

prospiciens summa placidum caput extulit unda.

Disiectam Aeneae toto videt aequore classem,

fluctibus oppressos Troas caelique ruina;

130 Nec latuere doli fratrem Iunonis et irae.

Eurum ad se Zephyrumque vocat, dehinc talia fatur:

"Tantane vos generis tenuit fiducia vestri?

Iam caelum terramque meo sine numine, venti,

miscere et tantas audetis tollere moles?

135 Quos ego—sed motos praestat componere fluctus.

Post mihi non simili poena commissa luetis.

Maturate fugam regique haec dicite vestro:

non illi imperium pelagi saevumque tridentem,

sed mihi sorte datum. Tenet ille immania saxa,

140 vestras, Eure, domos; illa se iactet in aula

Aeolus et clauso ventorum carcere regnet."

Sic ait, et dicto citius tumida aequora placat

collectasque fugat nubes solemque reducit.

Cymothoe simul et Triton adnixus acuto

145 detrudunt naves scopulo; levat ipse tridenti

et vastas aperit syrtes et temperat aequor

atque rotis summas levibus perlabitur undas.

Ac veluti magno in populo cum saepe coorta est

seditio saevitque animis ignobile vulgus

150 iamque faces et saxa volant, furor arma ministrat;

tum, pietate gravem ac meritis si forte virum quem

conspexere, silent arrectisque auribus astant;

ille regit dictis animos et pectora mulcet:

sic cunctus pelagi cecidit fragor, aequora postquam

155 prospiciens genitor caeloque invectus aperto

flectit equos curruque volans dat lora secundo.

Defessi Aeneadae quae proxima litora cursu

contendunt petere, et Libyae vertuntur ad oras.

Est in secessu longo locus: insula portum

160 efficit obiectu laterum, quibus omnis ab alto

frangitur inque sinus scindit sese unda reductos.

Hinc atque hinc vastae rupes geminique minantur

in caelum scopuli, quorum sub vertice late

aequora tuta silent; tum silvis scaena coruscis

165 desuper, horrentique atrum nemus imminet umbra.

Fronte sub adversa scopulis pendentibus antrum;

intus aquae dulces vivoque sedilia saxo,

Nympharum domus. hic fessas non vincula naves

ulla tenent, unco non alligat ancora morsu.

170 Huc septem Aeneas collectis navibus omni

ex numero subit, ac magno telluris amore

egressi optata potiuntur Troes harena

et sale tabentes artus in litore ponunt.

Ac primum silici scintillam excudit Achates

175 suscepitque ignem foliis atque arida circum

nutrimenta dedit rapuitque in fomite flammam.

Tum Cererem corruptam undis Cerealiaque arma

expediunt fessi rerum, frugesque receptas

et torrere parant flammis et frangere saxo.

180 Aeneas scopulum interea conscendit, et omnem

prospectum late pelago petit, Anthea si quem

iactatum vento videat Phrygiasque biremes

aut Capyn aut celsis in puppibus arma Caici.

Navem in conspectu nullam, tres litore cervos

185 prospicit errantes; hos tota armenta sequuntur

a tergo et longum per valles pascitur agmen.

Constitit hic arcumque manu celeresque sagittas

corripuit fidus quae tela gerebat Achates,

ductoresque ipsos primum capita alta ferentes

190 cornibus arboreis sternit, tum vulgus et omnem

miscet agens telis nemora inter frondea turbam;

nec prius absistit quam septem ingentia victor

corpora fundat humi et numerum cum navibus aequet;

hinc portum petit et socios partitur in omnes.

195 Vina bonus quae deinde cadis onerarat Acestes

litore Trinacrio dederatque abeuntibus heros

dividit, et dictis maerentia pectora mulcet:

"O socii (neque enim ignari sumus ante malorum),

O passi graviora, dabit deus his quoque finem.

200 Vos et Scyllaeam rabiem penitusque sonantes

accestis scopulos, vos et Cyclopia saxa

experti: revocate animos maestumque timorem

mittite; forsan et haec olim meminisse iuvabit.

Per varios casus, per tot discrimina rerum

205 tendimus in Latium, sedes ubi fata quietas

ostendunt; illic fas regna resurgere Troiae.

Durate, et vosmet rebus servate secundis."

Talia voce refert curisque ingentibus aeger

spem vultu simulat, premit altum corde dolorem.

Book 1.418–440

Corripuere viam interea, qua semita monstrat.

Iamque ascendebant collem, qui plurimus urbi

420 imminet adversasque aspectat desuper arces.

Miratur molem Aeneas, magalia quondam,

miratur portas strepitumque et strata viarum.

Instant ardentes Tyrii: pars ducere muros

molirique arcem et manibus subvolvere saxa,

425 pars optare locum tecto et concludere sulco;

iura magistratusque legunt sanctumque senatum.

Hic portus alii effodiunt; hic alta theatris

fundamenta locant alii, immanesque columnas

rupibus excidunt, scaenis decora alta futuris.

430 Qualis apes aestate nova per florea rura

exercet sub sole labor, cum gentis adultos

educunt fetus, aut cum liquentia mella

stipant et dulci distendunt nectare cellas,

aut onera accipiunt venientum, aut agmine facto

435 ignavum fucos pecus a praesepibus arcent;

fervet opus redolentque thymo fraglantia mella.

"O fortunati, quorum iam moenia surgunt!"

Aeneas ait et fastigia suspicit urbis.

Infert se saeptus nebula (mirabile dictu)

440   per medios, miscetque viris neque cernitur ulli.

BOOK 1.494–578

Haec dum Dardanio Aeneae miranda videntur,

495 dum stupet obtutuque haeret defixus in uno,

regina ad templum, forma pulcherrima Dido,

incessit magna iuvenum stipante caterva.

Qualis in Eurotae ripis aut per iuga Cynthi

exercet Diana choros, quam mille secutae

500 hinc atque hinc glomerantur Oreades; illa pharetram

fert umero gradiensque deas supereminet omnes

(Latonae tacitum pertemptant gaudia pectus):

talis erat Dido, talem se laeta ferebat

per medios instans operi regnisque futuris.

505 Tum foribus divae, media testudine templi,

saepta armis solioque alte subnixa resedit.

Iura dabat legesque viris, operumque laborem

partibus aequabat iustis aut sorte trahebat:

cum subito Aeneas concursu accedere magno

510 Anthea Sergestumque videt fortemque Cloanthum

Teucrorumque alios, ater quos aequore turbo

dispulerat penitusque alias avexerat oras.

Obstipuit simul ipse, simul percussus Achates

laetitiaque metuque; avidi coniungere dextras

515 ardebant, sed res animos incognita turbat.

Dissimulant et nube cava speculantur amicti

quae fortuna viris, classem quo litore linquant,

quid veniant; cunctis nam lecti navibus ibant

orantes veniam et templum clamore petebant.

520 Postquam introgressi et coram data copia fandi,

maximus Ilioneus placido sic pectore coepit:

"O regina, novam cui condere Iuppiter urbem

iustitiaque dedit gentes frenare superbas,

Troes te miseri, ventis maria omnia vecti,

525 oramus: prohibe infandos a navibus ignes,

parce pio generi et propius res aspice nostras.

Non nos aut ferro Libycos populare penates

venimus, aut raptas ad litora vertere praedas;

non ea vis animo nec tanta superbia victis.

530 Est locus, Hesperiam Grai cognomine dicunt,

terra antiqua, potens armis atque ubere glaebae;

Oenotri coluere viri; nunc fama minores

Italiam dixisse ducis de nomine gentem.

Hic cursus fuit,

535 cum subito adsurgens fluctu nimbosus Orion

in vada caeca tulit penitusque procacibus Austris

perque undas superante salo perque invia saxa

dispulit; huc pauci vestris adnavimus oris.

Quod genus hoc hominum? Quaeve hunc tam barbara morem

540 permittit patria? Hospitio prohibemur harenae;

bella cient primaque vetant consistere terra.

Si genus humanum et mortalia temnitis arma,

at sperate deos memores fandi atque nefandi.

Rex erat Aeneas nobis, quo iustior alter,

545 nec pietate fuit, nec bello maior et armis.

Quem si fata virum servant, si vescitur aura

aetheria neque adhuc crudelibus occubat umbris,

non metus, officio nec te certasse priorem

paeniteat. Sunt et Siculis regionibus urbes

550 armaque Troianoque a sanguine clarus Acestes.

Quassatam ventis liceat subducere classem

et silvis aptare trabes et stringere remos,

si datur Italiam sociis et rege recepto

tendere, ut Italiam laeti Latiumque petamus;

555 sin absumpta salus, et te, pater optime Teucrum,

pontus habet Libyae nec spes iam restat Iuli,

at freta Sicaniae saltem sedesque paratas,

unde huc adventi, regemque petamus Acesten."

Talibus Ilioneus; cuncti simul ore fremebant

560 Dardanidae.

Tum breviter Dido vultum demissa profatur:

"Solvite corde metum, Teucri, secludite curas.

Res dura et regni novitas me talia cogunt

moliri et late fines custode tueri.

565 Quis genus Aeneadum, quis Troiae nesciat urbem,

virtutesque virosque aut tanti incendia belli?

Non obtunsa adeo gestamus pectora Poeni,

nec tam aversus equos Tyria Sol iungit ab urbe.

Seu vos Hesperiam magnam Saturniaque arva

570 sive Erycis fines regemque optatis Acesten,

auxilio tutos dimittam opibusque iuvabo.

Vultis et his mecum pariter considere regnis?

Urbem quam statuo, vestra est; subducite naves;

Tros Tyriusque mihi nullo discrimine agetur.

575 Atque utinam rex ipse Noto compulsus eodem

adforet Aeneas! Equidem per litora certos

dimittam et Libyae lustrare extrema iubebo,

si quibus eiectus silvis aut urbibus errat."

Book 2

BOOK 2.40–56

40 Primus ibi ante omnes magna comitante caterva

Laocoon ardens summa decurrit ab arce,

et procul 'O miseri, quae tanta insania, cives?

Creditis avectos hostes? Aut ulla putatis

dona carere dolis Danaum? Sic notus Ulixes?

45 Aut hoc inclusi ligno occultantur Achivi,

aut haec in nostros fabricata est machina muros,

inspectura domos venturaque desuper urbi,

aut aliquis latet error; equo ne credite, Teucri.

Quidquid id est, timeo Danaos et dona ferentes.'

50 Sic fatus validis ingentem viribus hastam

in latus inque feri curvam compagibus alvum

contorsit. Stetit illa tremens, uteroque recusso

insonuere cavae gemitumque dedere cavernae.

Et, si fata deum, si mens non laeva fuisset,

55 impulerat ferro Argolicas foedare latebras,

Troiaque nunc staret, Priamique arx alta maneres.

Book 2.201–249

Laocoon, ductus Neptuno sorte sacerdos,

sollemnes taurum ingentem mactabat ad aras.

Ecce autem gemini a Tenedo tranquilla per alta

(horresco referens) immensis orbibus angues

205 incumbunt pelago pariterque ad litora tendunt;

pectora quorum inter fluctus arrecta iubaeque

sanguineae superant undas, pars cetera pontum

pone legit sinuatque immensa volumine terga.

Fit sonitus spumante salo; iamque arva tenebant

210 ardentesque oculos suffecti sanguine et igni

sibila lambebant linguis vibrantibus ora.

Diffugimus visu exsangues. Illi agmine certo

Laocoonta petunt; et primum parva duorum

corpora natorum serpens amplexus uterque

215 implicat et miseros morsu depascitur artus;

post ipsum auxilio subeuntem ac tela ferentem

corripiunt spirisque ligant ingentibus; et iam

bis medium amplexi, bis collo squamea circum

terga dati superant capite et cervicibus altis.

220 Ille simul manibus tendit divellere nodos

perfusus sanie vittas atroque veneno,

clamores simul horrendos ad sidera tollit:

qualis mugitus, fugit cum saucius aram

taurus et incertam excussit cervice securim.

225 At gemini lapsu delubra ad summa dracones

effugiunt saevaeque petunt Tritonidis arcem,

sub pedibusque deae clipeique sub orbe teguntur.

Tum vero tremefacta novus per pectora cunctis

insinuat pavor, et scelus expendisse merentem

230 Laocoonta ferunt, sacrum qui cuspide robur

laeserit et tergo sceleratam intorserit hastam.

Ducendum ad sedes simulacrum orandaque divae

numina conclamant.

Dividimus muros et moenia pandimus urbis.

235 Accingunt omnes operi pedibusque rotarum

subiciunt lapsus, et stuppea vincula collo

intendunt: scandit fatalis machina muros

feta armis. Pueri circum innuptaeque puellae

sacra canunt funemque manu contingere gaudent;

240 illa subit mediaeque minans inlabitur urbi.

O patria, O divum domus Ilium et incluta bello

moenia Dardanidum! quater ipso in limine portae

substitit atque utero sonitum quater arma dedere;

instamus tamen immemores caecique furore

245 et monstrum infelix sacrata sistimus arce.

Tunc etiam fatis aperit Cassandra futuris

ora dei iussu non umquam credita Teucris.

Nos delubra deum miseri, quibus ultimus esset

ille dies, festa velamus fronde per urbem.

Book 2.268–297

Tempus erat quo prima quies mortalibus aegris

incipit et dono divum gratissima serpit.

270 In somnis, ecce, ante oculos maestissimus Hector

visus adesse mihi largosque effundere fletus,

raptatus bigis ut quondam, aterque cruento

pulvere perque pedes traiectus lora tumentes.

Ei mihi, qualis erat, quantum mutatus ab illo

275 Hectore qui redit exuvias indutus Achilli

vel Danaum Phrygios iaculatus puppibus ignes;

squalentem barbam et concretos sanguine crines

vulneraque illa gerens, quae circum plurima muros

accepit patrios. Ultro flens ipse videbar

280 compellare virum et maestas expromere voces:

'O lux Dardaniae, spes O fidissima Teucrum,

quae tantae tenuere morae? Quibus Hector ab oris

exspectate venis? Ut te post multa tuorum

funera, post varios hominumque urbisque labores

285 defessi aspicimus! Quae causa indigna serenos

foedavit vultus? Aut cur haec vulnera cerno?'

Ille nihil, nec me quaerentem vana moratur,

sed graviter gemitus imo de pectore ducens,

'Heu fuge, nate dea, teque his' ait 'eripe flammis.

290   Hostis habet muros; ruit alto a culmine Troia.

Sat patriae Priamoque datum: si Pergama dextra

defendi possent, etiam hac defensa fuissent.

Sacra suosque tibi commendat Troia penates;

hos cape fatorum comites, his moenia quaere

295   magna, pererrato statues quae denique ponto.'

Sic ait et manibus vittas Vestamque potentem

aeternumque adytis effert penetralibus ignem.

Book 2.559–620

At me tum primum saevus circumstetit horror.

560 Obstipui; subiit cari genitoris imago,

ut regem aequaevum crudeli vulnere vidi

vitam exhalantem, subiit deserta Creusa

et direpta domus et parvi casus Iuli.

Respicio et quae sit me circum copia lustro.

565 Deseruere omnes defessi, et corpora saltu

ad terram misere aut ignibus aegra dedere.

[Iamque adeo super unus eram, cum limina Vestae

servantem et tacitam secreta in sede latentem

Tyndarida aspicio; dant claram incendia lucem

570 erranti passimque oculos per cuncta ferenti.

Illa sibi infestos eversa ob Pergama Teucros

et Danaum poenam et deserti coniugis iras

praemetuens, Troiae et patriae communis Erinys,

abdiderat sese atque aris invisa sedebat.

575 Exarsere ignes animo; subit ira cadentem

ulcisci patriam et sceleratas sumere poenas.

"Scilicet haec Spartam incolumis patriasque Mycenas

aspiciet, partoque ibit regina triumpho?

Coniugiumque domumque patris natosque videbit

580 Iliadum turba et Phrygiis comitata ministris?

Occiderit ferro Priamus? Troia arserit igni?

Dardanium totiens sudarit sanguine litus?

Non ita. Namque etsi nullum memorabile nomen

feminea in poena est, habet haec victoria laudem;

585 exstinxisse nefas tamen et sumpsisse merentes

laudabor poenas, animumque explesse iuvabit

ultricis †famam et cineres satiasse meorum."

Talia iactabam et furiata mente ferebar,]

cum mihi se, non ante oculis tam clara, videndam

590 obtulit et pura per noctem in luce refulsit

alma parens, confessa deam qualisque videri

caelicolis et quanta solet, dextraque prehensum

continuit roseoque haec insuper addidit ore:

" Nate, quis indomitas tantus dolor excitat iras?

595 Quid furis? Aut quonam nostri tibi cura recessit?

Non prius aspicies ubi fessum aetate parentem

liqueris Anchisen, superet coniunxne Creusa

Ascaniusque puer? Quos omnes undique Graiae

circum errant acies et, ni mea cura resistat,

600 iam flammae tulerint inimicus et hauserit ensis.

Non tibi Tyndaridis facies invisa Lacaenae

culpatusve Paris, divum inclementia, divum

has evertit opes sternitque a culmine Troiam.

Aspice (namque omnem, quae nunc obducta tuenti

605 mortales hebetat visus tibi et umida circum

caligat, nubem eripiam; tu ne qua parentis

iussa time neu praeceptis parere recusa):

hic, ubi disiectas moles avulsaque saxis

saxa vides, mixtoque undantem pulvere fumum,

610 eptunus muros magnoque emota tridenti

fundamenta quatit totamque a sedibus urbem

eruit. Hic Iuno Scaeas saevissima portas

prima tenet sociumque furens a navibus agmen

ferro accincta vocat.

615 Iam summas arces Tritonia, respice, Pallas

insedit nimbo effulgens et Gorgone saeva.

Ipse pater Danais animos viresque secundas

sufficit, ipse deos in Dardana suscitat arma.

Eripe, nate, fugam finemque impone labori;

620 nusquam abero et tutum patrio te limine sistam.'

Book 4

BOOK 4.160–218

160 Interea magno misceri murmure caelum

incipit, insequitur commixta grandine nimbus,

et Tyrii comites passim et Troiana iuventus

Dardaniusque nepos Veneris diversa per agros

tecta metu petiere; ruunt de montibus amnes.

165 Speluncam Dido dux et Troianus eandem

deveniunt. Prima et Tellus et pronuba Iuno

dant signum; fulsere ignes et conscius aether

conubiis summoque ulularunt vertice Nymphae.

Ille dies primus leti primusque malorum

170 causa fuit; neque enim specie famave movetur

nec iam furtivum Dido meditatur amorem:

coniugium vocat, hoc praetexit nomine culpam.

Extemplo Libyae magnas it Fama per urbes,

Fama, malum qua non aliud velocius ullum:

175 mobilitate viget viresque adquirit eundo,

parva metu primo, mox sese attollit in auras

ingrediturque solo et caput inter nubila condit.

Illam Terra parens ira inritata deorum

extremam, ut perhibent, Coeo Enceladoque sororem

180 progenuit pedibus celerem et pernicibus alis,

monstrum horrendum, ingens, cui quot sunt corpore plumae,

tot vigiles oculi subter (mirabile dictu),

tot linguae, totidem ora sonant, tot subrigit aures.

Nocte volat caeli medio terraeque per umbram

185 stridens, nec dulci declinat lumina somno;

luce sedet custos aut summi culmine tecti

turribus aut altis, et magnas territat urbes,

tam ficti pravique tenax quam nuntia veri.

Haec tum multiplici populos sermone replebat

190 gaudens, et pariter facta atque infecta canebat:

venisse Aenean Troiano sanguine cretum,

cui se pulchra viro dignetur iungere Dido;

nunc hiemem inter se luxu, quam longa, fovere

regnorum immemores turpique cupidine captos.

195 Haec passim dea foeda virum diffundit in ora.

Protinus ad regem cursus detorquet Iarban

incenditque animum dictis atque aggerat iras.

Hic Hammone satus rapta Garamantide nympha

templa Iovi centum latis immania regnis,

200 centum aras posuit vigilemque sacraverat ignem,

excubias divum aeternas, pecudumque cruore

pingue solum et variis florentia limina sertis.

Isque amens animi et rumore accensus amaro

dicitur ante aras media inter numina divum

205 multa Iovem manibus supplex orasse supinis:

"Iuppiter omnipotens, cui nunc Maurusia pictis

gens epulata toris Lenaeum libat honorem,

aspicis haec? An te, genitor, cum fulmina torques

nequiquam horremus, caecique in nubibus ignes

210 terrificant animos et inania murmura miscent?

Femina, quae nostris errans in finibus urbem

exiguam pretio posuit, cui litus arandum

cuique loci leges dedimus, conubia nostra

reppulit ac dominum Aenean in regna recepit.

215 Et nunc ille Paris cum semiviro comitatu,

Maeonia mentum mitra crinemque madentem

subnexus, rapto potitur: nos munera templis

quippe tuis ferimus famamque fovemus inanem."

BOOK 4.259–361

Ut primum alatis tetigit magalia plantis,

260 Aenean fundantem arces ac tecta novantem

conspicit. Atque illi stellatus iaspide fulva

ensis erat Tyrioque ardebat murice laena

demissa ex umeris, dives quae munera Dido

fecerat, et tenui telas discreverat auro.

265 Continuo invadit: "Tu nunc Karthaginis altae

fundamenta locas pulchramque uxorius urbem

exstruis? Heu, regni rerumque oblite tuarum!

Ipse deum tibi me claro demittit Olympo

regnator, caelum et terras qui numine torquet,

270 ipse haec ferre iubet celeres mandata per auras:

Quid struis? Aut qua spe Libycis teris otia terris?

Si te nulla movet tantarum gloria rerum

[nec super ipse tua moliris laude laborem,]

Ascanium surgentem et spes heredis Iuli

275 respice, cui regnum Italiae Romanaque tellus

debetur." Tali Cyllenius ore locutus

mortales visus medio sermone reliquit

et procul in tenuem ex oculis evanuit auram.

At vero Aeneas aspectu obmutuit amens,

280   arrectaeque horrore comae et vox faucibus haesit.

Ardet abire fuga dulcesque relinquere terras,

attonitus tanto monitu imperioque deorum.

Heu quid agat? Quo nunc reginam ambire furentem

audeat adfatu? Quae prima exordia sumat?

285   Atque animum nunc huc celerem nunc dividit illuc

in partesque rapit varias perque omnia versat.

Haec alternanti potior sententia visa est:

Mnesthea Sergestumque vocat fortemque Serestum,

classem aptent taciti sociosque ad litora cogant,

290   arma parent et quae rebus sit causa novandis

dissimulent; sese interea, quando optima Dido

nesciat et tantos rumpi non speret amores,

temptaturum aditus et quae mollissima fandi

tempora, quis rebus dexter modus. Ocius omnes

295   imperio laeti parent et iussa facessunt.

At regina dolos (quis fallere possit amantem?)

praesensit, motusque excepit prima futuros

omnia tuta timens. Eadem impia Fama furenti

detulit armari classem cursumque parari.

300   Saevit inops animi totamque incensa per urbem

bacchatur, qualis commotis excita sacris

Thyias, ubi audito stimulant trieterica Baccho

orgia nocturnusque vocat clamore Cithaeron.

Tandem his Aenean compellat vocibus ultro:

305 "Dissimulare etiam sperasti, perfide, tantum

posse nefas tacitusque mea decedere terra?

Nec te noster amor nec te data dextera quondam

nec moritura tenet crudeli funere Dido?

Quin etiam hiberno moliri sidere classem

310 et mediis properas Aquilonibus ire per altum,

crudelis? Quid, si non arva aliena domosque

ignotas peteres, et Troia antiqua maneret,

Troia per undosum peteretur classibus aequor?

Mene fugis? Per ego has lacrimas dextramque tuam te

315 (quando aliud mihi iam miserae nihil ipsa reliqui),

per conubia nostra, per inceptos hymenaeos,

si bene quid de te merui, fuit aut tibi quicquam

dulce meum, miserere domus labentis et istam,

oro, si quis adhuc precibus locus, exue mentem.

320 Te propter Libycae gentes Nomadumque tyranni

odere, infensi Tyrii; te propter eundem

exstinctus pudor et, qua sola sidera adibam,

fama prior. Cui me moribundam deseris hospes

(hoc solum nomen quoniam de coniuge restat)?

325 Quid moror? An mea Pygmalion dum moenia frater

destruat aut captam ducat Gaetulus Iarbas?

Saltem si qua mihi de te suscepta fuisset

ante fugam suboles, si quis mihi parvulus aula

luderet Aeneas, qui te tamen ore referret,

330 non equidem omnino capta ac deserta viderer."

Dixerat. Ille Iovis monitis immota tenebat

lumina et obnixus curam sub corde premebat.

Tandem pauca refert: "Ego te, quae plurima fando

enumerare vales, numquam, regina, negabo

335 promeritam, nec me meminisse pigebit Elissae

dum memor ipse mei, dum spiritus hos regit artus.

Pro re pauca loquar. Neque ego hanc abscondere furto

speravi (ne finge) fugam, nec coniugis umquam

praetendi taedas aut haec in foedera veni.

340 Me si fata meis paterentur ducere vitam

auspiciis et sponte mea componere curas,

urbem Troianam primum dulcesque meorum

reliquias colerem, Priami tecta alta manerent,

et recidiva manu posuissem Pergama victis.

345 Sed nunc Italiam magnam Gryneus Apollo,

Italiam Lyciae iussere capessere sortes;

hic amor, haec patria est. si te Karthaginis arces

Phoenissam Libycaeque aspectus detinet urbis,

quae tandem Ausonia Teucros considere terra

350 invidia est? Et nos fas extera quaerere regna.

Me patris Anchisae, quotiens umentibus umbris

nox operit terras, quotiens astra ignea surgunt,

admonet in somnis et turbida terret imago;

me puer Ascanius capitisque iniuria cari,

355 quem regno Hesperiae fraudo et fatalibus arvis.

Nunc etiam interpres divum Iove missus ab ipso

(testor utrumque caput) celeres mandata per auras

detulit: ipse deum manifesto in lumine vidi

intrantem muros vocemque his auribus hausi.

360 Desine meque tuis incendere teque querelis;

Italiam non sponte sequor."

Book 4.659–705

Dixit, et os impressa toro "Moriemur inultae,

660 sed moriamur" ait. "Sic, sic iuvat ire sub umbras.

Hauriat hunc oculis ignem crudelis ab alto

Dardanus, et nostrae secum ferat omina mortis."

Dixerat, atque illam media inter talia ferro

conlapsam aspiciunt comites, ensemque cruore

665 spumantem sparsasque manus. It clamor ad alta

atria: concussam bacchatur Fama per urbem.

Lamentis gemituque et femineo ululatu

tecta fremunt, resonat magnis plangoribus aether,

non aliter quam si immissis ruat hostibus omnis

670 Karthago aut antiqua Tyros, flammaeque furentes

culmina perque hominum volvantur perque deorum.

Audiit exanimis trepidoque exterrita cursu

unguibus ora soror foedans et pectora pugnis

per medios ruit, ac morientem nomine clamat:

675 "Hoc illud, germana, fuit? Me fraude petebas?

Hoc rogus iste mihi, hoc ignes araeque parabant?

Quid primum deserta querar? Comitemne sororem

sprevisti moriens? Eadem me ad fata vocasses:

idem ambas ferro dolor atque eadem hora tulisset.

680 His etiam struxi manibus patriosque vocavi

voce deos, sic te ut posita, crudelis, abessem?

Exstinxti te meque, soror, populumque patresque

Sidonios urbemque tuam. Date, vulnera lymphis

abluam et, extremus si quis super halitus errat,

685 ore legam." Sic fata gradus evaserat altos,

semianimemque sinu germanam amplexa fovebat

cum gemitu atque atros siccabat veste cruores.

Illa graves oculos conata attollere rursus

deficit; infixum stridit sub pectore vulnus.

690 Ter sese attollens cubitoque adnixa levavit,

ter revoluta toro est oculisque errantibus alto

quaesivit caelo lucem ingemuitque reperta.

Tum Iuno omnipotens longum miserata dolorem

difficilesque obitus Irim demisit Olympo

695 quae luctantem animam nexosque resolveret artus.

Nam quia nec fato merita nec morte peribat,

sed misera ante diem subitoque accensa furore,

nondum illi flavum Proserpina vertice crinem

abstulerat Stygioque caput damnaverat Orco.

700 Ergo Iris croceis per caelum roscida pennis

mille trahens varios adverso sole colores

devolat et supra caput astitit. "Hunc ego Diti

sacrum iussa fero teque isto corpore solvo":

Sic ait et dextra crinem secat, omnis et una

705 dilapsus calor atque in ventos vita recessit.

Book 6

Book 6.295–332

295 Hinc via Tartarei quae fert Acherontis ad undas.

Turbidus hic caeno vastaque voragine gurges

aestuat atque omnem Cocŷto eructat harenam.

Portitor has horrendus aquas et flumina servat

terribili squalore Charon, cui plurima mento

300 canities inculta iacet, stant lumina flamma,

sordidus ex umeris nodo dependet amictus.

Ipse ratem conto subigit velisque ministrat

et ferruginea subvectat corpora cumba,

iam senior, sed cruda deo viridisque senectus.

305 Huc omnis turba ad ripas effusa ruebat,

matres atque viri defunctaque corpora vita

magnanimum heroum, pueri innuptaeque puellae,

impositique rogis iuvenes ante ora parentum:

quam multa in silvis autumni frigore primo

310 lapsa cadunt folia, aut ad terram gurgite ab alto

quam multae glomerantur aves, ubi frigidus annus

trans pontum fugat et terris immittit apricis.

Stabant orantes primi transmittere cursum

tendebantque manus ripae ulterioris amore.

₃₁₅ Navita sed tristis nunc hos nunc accipit illos,

ast alios longe summotos arcet harena.

Aeneas miratus enim motusque tumultu

"Dic," ait, "o virgo, quid vult concursus ad amnem?

Quidve petunt animae? Vel quo discrimine ripas

₃₂₀ hae linquunt, illae remis vada livida verrunt?"

Olli sic breviter fata est longaeva sacerdos:

"Anchisa generate, deum certissima proles,

Cocŷti stagna alta vides Stygiamque paludem,

di cuius iurare timent et fallere numen.

₃₂₅ Haec omnis, quam cernis, inops inhumataque turba est;

portitor ille Charon; hi, quos vehit unda, sepulti.

Nec ripas datur horrendas et rauca fluenta

transportare prius quam sedibus ossa quierunt.

Centum errant annos volitantque haec litora circum;

₃₃₀ tum demum admissi stagna exoptata revisunt."

Constitit Anchisa satus et vestigia pressit

multa putans sortemque animo miseratus iniquam.

BOOK 6.384–425

Ergo iter inceptum peragunt fluvioque propinquant.

385   Navita quos iam inde ut Stygia prospexit ab unda

per tacitum nemus ire pedemque advertere ripae,

sic prior adgreditur dictis atque increpat ultro:

"Quisquis es, armatus qui nostra ad flumina tendis,

fare age, quid venias, iam istinc et comprime gressum.

390   Umbrarum hic locus est, somni noctisque soporae:

corpora viva nefas Stygia vectare carina.

Nec vero Alciden me sum laetatus euntem

accepisse lacu, nec Thesea Pirithoümque,

dis quamquam geniti atque invicti viribus essent.

395   Tartareum ille manu custodem in vincla petivit

ipsius a solio regis traxitque trementem;

hi dominam Ditis thalamo deducere adorti."

Quae contra breviter fata est Amphrŷsia vates:

'Nullae hic insidiae tales (absiste moveri),

400   nec vim tela ferunt; licet ingens ianitor antro

aeternum latrans exsangues terreat umbras,

casta licet patrui servet Proserpina limen.

Troius Aeneas, pietate insignis et armis,

ad genitorem imas Erebi descendit ad umbras.

405   Si te nulla movet tantae pietatis imago,

at ramum hunc" (aperit ramum qui veste latebat)

" agnoscas." Tumida ex ira tum corda residunt;

nec plura his. Ille admirans venerabile donum

fatalis virgae longo post tempore visum

410   caeruleam advertit puppim ripaeque propinquat.

Inde alias animas, quae per iuga longa sedebant,

deturbat laxatque foros; simul accipit alveo

ingentem Aenean. Gemuit sub pondere cumba

sutilis et multam accepit rimosa paludem.

415   Tandem trans fluvium incolumes vatemque virumque

informi limo glaucaque exponit in ulva.

Cerberus haec ingens latratu regna trifauci

personat adverso recubans immanis in antro.

Cui vates horrere videns iam colla colubris

420   melle soporatam et medicatis frugibus offam

obicit. Ille fame rabida tria guttura pandens

corripit obiectam, atque immania terga resolvit

fusus humi totoque ingens extenditur antro.

Occupat Aeneas aditum custode sepulto

425   evaditque celer ripam inremeabilis undae.

BOOK 6.450–76

450 Inter quas Phoenissa recens a vulnere Dido

errabat silva in magna; quam Troius heros

ut primum iuxta stetit agnovitque per umbras

obscuram, qualem primo qui surgere mense

aut videt aut vidisse putat per nubila lunam,

455 demisit lacrimas dulcique adfatus amore est:

"Infelix Dido, verus mihi nuntius ergo

venerat exstinctam ferroque extrema secutam?

Funeris heu tibi causa fui? Per sidera iuro,

per superos et si qua fides tellure sub ima est,

460 invitus, regina, tuo de litore cessi.

Sed me iussa deum, quae nunc has ire per umbras,

per loca senta situ cogunt noctemque profundam,

imperiis egere suis; nec credere quivi

hunc tantum tibi me discessu ferre dolorem.

465 Siste gradum teque aspectu ne subtrahe nostro.

Quem fugis? Extremum fato quod te adloquor hoc est."

Talibus Aeneas ardentem et torva tuentem

lenibat dictis animum lacrimasque ciebat.

Illa solo fixos oculos aversa tenebat

470 nec magis incepto vultum sermone movetur

quam si dura silex aut stet Marpesia cautes.

Tandem corripuit sese atque inimica refugit

in nemus umbriferum, coniunx ubi pristinus illi

respondet curis aequatque Sychaeus amorem.

475 Nec minus Aeneas casu concussus iniquo

prosequitur lacrimis longe et miseratur euntem.

Book 6.847–901

"Excudent alii spirantia mollius aera

(credo equidem), vivos ducent de marmore vultus,

orabunt causas melius, caelique meatus

850 describent radio et surgentia sidera dicent:

tu regere imperio populos, Romane, memento

(hae tibi erunt artes), pacique imponere morem,

parcere subiectis et debellare superbos."

Sic pater Anchises, atque haec mirantibus addit:

855 "Aspice, ut insignis spoliis Marcellus opimis

ingreditur victorque viros supereminet omnes.

Hic rem Romanam magno turbante tumultu

sistet eques, sternet Poenos Gallumque rebellem,

tertiaque arma patri suspendet capta Quirino."

860 Atque hic Aeneas (una namque ire videbat

egregium forma iuvenem et fulgentibus armis,

sed frons laeta parum et deiecto lumina vultu)

"Quis, pater, ille, virum qui sic comitatur euntem?

Filius, anne aliquis magna de stirpe nepotum?

865 Qui strepitus circa comitum! Quantum instar in ipso!

Sed nox atra caput tristi circumvolat umbra."

Tum pater Anchises lacrimis ingressus obortis:

"O gnate, ingentem luctum ne quaere tuorum;

ostendent terris hunc tantum fata neque ultra

870 esse sinent. Nimium vobis Romana propago

visa potens, superi, propria haec si dona fuissent.

Quantos ille virum magnam Mavortis ad urbem

campus aget gemitus! Vel quae, Tiberine, videbis

funera, cum tumulum praeterlabere recentem!

875 Nec puer Iliaca quisquam de gente Latinos

in tantum spe tollet avos, nec Romula quondam

ullo se tantum tellus iactabit alumno.

Heu pietas, heu prisca fides invictaque bello

dextera! Non illi se quisquam impune tulisset

880 obvius armato, seu cum pedes iret in hostem

seu spumantis equi foderet calcaribus armos.

Heu, miserande puer, si qua fata aspera rumpas—

tu Marcellus eris. Manibus date lilia plenis

purpureos spargam flores animamque nepotis

885 his saltem accumulem donis, et fungar inani

munere." Sic tota passim regione vagantur

aeris in campis latis atque omnia lustrant.

Quae postquam Anchises natum per singula duxit

incenditque animum famae venientis amore,

890   exim bella viro memorat quae deinde gerenda,

Laurentesque docet populos urbemque Latini,

et quo quemque modo fugiatque feratque laborem.

Sunt geminae Somni portae, quarum altera fertur

cornea, qua veris facilis datur exitus umbris,

895   altera candenti perfecta nitens elephanto,

sed falsa ad caelum mittunt insomnia Manes.

His ibi tum natum Anchises unaque Sibyllam

prosequitur dictis portaque emittit eburna;

ille viam secat ad naves sociosque revisit.